Pearson Test of English **General**

Pearson English International Certificate

1

Practice Tests **Plus**

Level **1** (A2)

with **key** and
Teacher's Resources

CONTENTS

TEST OVERVIEW

The **Pearson Test of English General**, paper-based test, Level 1 (otherwise known as **PTE General** or **Pearson English International Certificate**), is an accredited ESOL International qualification at A2 level. The test is designed to assess test taker's four main skills in English (Reading, Listening, Writing and Speaking) through a variety of real-life tasks; from writing in different formats and understanding a variety of spoken and written materials, to participating in conversations. The test taker's skills are tested in all four skills areas, according to the descriptors outlined in the *Common European Framework of Reference for Languages* (CEFR) at an A2 level.

The test has two parts; a written paper and a Speaking test. In the written paper, test takers must complete tasks that assess their Listening, Reading and Writing skills. The Speaking test assesses test taker's communicative abilities in three different situations.

Part 1: Written Test

The written paper is divided into nine sections, each section focusing on a different skill area. The total time for completing this paper is 1 hour and 15 minutes. The total possible scores for Sections 1–9 is 75 points.

Section	Task	Skills Tested and Objectives	Task description	Score points
1	3-option graphical multiple choice	**Listening** Assesses ability to understand the gist of short spoken utterances.	Test takers listen once to ten short recordings and answer a single question for each by choosing which of three pictures matches what is heard. There are ten questions to answer; one per recording.	10
2	Dictation	**Listening and Writing** Assesses ability to understand a short utterance by transcribing a spoken text.	Test takers listen to one person speaking and write exactly what is heard with correct spellings. The extract is played twice, the second time with pauses, giving time to write down word-for-word what is heard. There is one dictation to complete and one recording.	5 Listening 5 Writing
3	Text/note completion	**Listening** Assesses ability to extract specific information from spoken texts.	Test takers listen twice to two texts and complete sentences, notes or a continuous text for each using the information heard. There are ten gaps to complete; five per recording.	10
4	Gap fill, 3-option multiple choice	**Reading** Assesses ability to understand the purpose, structure and main idea of short written texts.	Test takers read five short texts, each containing a gap, and choose which of three answer options is the missing word or phrase. There are five gaps to complete; one per text.	5
5	3-option graphical multiple choice	**Reading** Assesses ability to understand the main detail in short written texts.	Test takers read five short texts. For each test they must select the picture which matches the content of the text from three answer options.	5
6	Open-ended question	**Reading** Assesses ability to understand the main points of short written texts.	Test takers read two texts and answer eight questions about them using single words or short answers. There are four questions per text to respond to.	8

TEST OVERVIEW

Section	Task	Skills Tested and Objectives	Task description	Score points
7	Text/note completion	**Reading** Assesses ability to extract specific information from a written text.	Test takers read a text and use information from it to fill seven gaps in an incomplete text or notes. There are seven gaps to complete, one source text and a set of notes.	7
8	Write correspondence	**Writing** Assesses ability to write a short piece of correspondence (50–70 words).	Test takers write a short email or letter, etc. based on information given in Section 7. There is one text to write (50–70 words).	10
9	Write text	**Writing** Assesses ability to write a short text based on a picture (80–100 words).	Test takers write a short text based on a visual image. They choose one of two sets of pictures. The form of the response may be a diary entry, short story or description. There is one text to write (80–100 words).	10

Part 2: Speaking Paper

The Speaking test is divided into three sections at Level 1 (A2), which are Sections 10, 12 and 13. Each section focuses on a different speaking skills and abilities.

During this part of the test, a test taker sits with an examiner.

The total time for completing this paper is 5 minutes and each section has its own time limits.

The total possible scores for Sections 10, 12 and 13 is 25 points.

Section	Task	Skills Tested and Objectives	Task description	Score points
10	Sustained monologue (1.5 minutes)	**Speaking** Assesses ability to speak about matters of personal information and interest.	Test takers speak about personal information and interests in response to questions posed by the examiner.	25 score points in total; distributed across the marking criteria
12	Describe picture (2 minutes)	**Speaking** Assesses ability to speak about a picture.	Test takers describe a picture in response to questions posed by the examiner.	
13	Role play (1.5 minutes)	**Speaking** Assesses ability to perform and respond to basic language functions appropriately.	Test takers take part in a role play with the interlocutor using a role card with information and instructions.	

INTRODUCTION

Print book 📖

- This book contains five complete practice tests, which are modelled on the task types in the **Pearson Test of English General** (*Pearson English International Certificate*).

- **Test 1** provides specific guidance and tips for each section of the test and its tasks. This is done through an *Overview* of each skill section (listening, reading, writing and speaking), *How to* pages that give students tips and guidance on approaching each section task and *Training* pages where students can practice with the tasks in Test 1 with additional guidance and support.

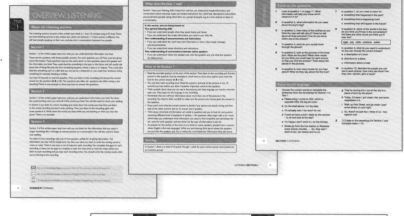

- **Test 2** provides tip strips, which give detailed support with each task in the test. Tips are focused on specific questions and help students to learn about what they need to do to answer them.

- **Tests 3–5** are practice tests without support or tips. These are for students to practice with each task type on their own.

- **Visuals for the Speaking Test** pages, located at the back of the book, are where students can find all the visual aids and examiner role cards they will need to practice the speaking tasks. Use these to teach students about the kinds of materials they will see in the speaking sections of the test or to practise doing the task types.

- **Speaking banks** at the back of the book, offer **detailed guidance** on Sections 10–13 of the test. These pages feature **speaking tasks from the tests**, give helpful *Test Tips*, *Useful Language* and practice activities to help students prepare for the Speaking test.

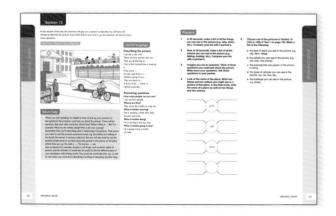

- **Writing banks** at the back of the book, offer **detailed guidance** on the tasks in Sections 8 and 9 of the written paper. These pages feature **writing tasks from the tests** and some *Sample Answers*. You can also find *Test Tips*, *Useful Language* and ideas for *Planning your writing* in this section. The pages provide a writing *Checklist* for each type of text featured, as well as *Practice Activities* to help students prepare.

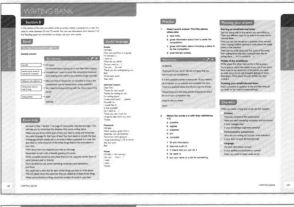

- A **Grammar bank** at the back of the book, has grammar explanations and practice activities at A2 level for extra revision.

- At the end of the Speaking and Writing banks there is information and tips for students on *How to prepare* themselves for Sections 8–13 of the test.

Online Resources

The additional resources which support the book are available online on the *Pearson English Portal* at **https://pearson.com/english/portal.html**.

These resources include:

- **Audio** to accompany the tasks in the book and **audio scripts**.
- Full **answer keys** for all test 1–5 tasks, training activities and Speaking, Writing and Grammar banks.
- **Speaking videos** of a student and an examiner doing the speaking sections of the test, as well as **worksheets** for students to use while watching and teacher's notes.
- **Expert feedback** on the speaking videos and the student's performance.
- **Writing worksheets** with teacher's notes, focused on writing forms introduced in the book.
- **Vocabulary maps** with topics covered in the book.
- **Teaching notes** with classroom ideas for each section of the test.
- A **PTE General Scoring Guide** for this level, as well as **Writing and Speaking Criteria**, including an overview of the speaking and writing skills assessed by test level.
- A **Teacher's Guide to the Computer Based Test**.

Pearson Practice English App

You can also find **PTE General** resources for practice on the *Pearson Practice English* app. Create an account using your access code via the *Pearson English Portal* or directly on the app on a mobile device. The resources available include:

- **Audio** from the book
- **Speaking Test Videos**
- **Additional practice** with 280 vocabulary items, taken from the topics covered in the book.

Ready test

If you would like to see how you might perform in the **Pearson Test of English General**, go to the **Ready Test** at **english.com/readytest** and take a test to find out! The test will be launched in Autumn 2020!

OVERVIEW: LISTENING

About the Listening sections

The Listening sections are part of the written test which is 1 hour 35 minutes long at A2 level. There are three listening sections in the written test, which are Sections 1–3. Each section is different. You will hear people speaking on their own, and also short conversations between two people.

Section 1

Section 1 of the written paper tests how well you can understand the information you hear.

There are ten questions with three possible answers. For each question, you will hear a person giving some information. These questions may be *who, what, where* or *how* questions about the speaker and the information you hear. They could describe something in the past or the future and will usually talk about lots of things like jobs, the time something happens, where a place is or objects. They could also describe something, such as a dish that you can eat at a restaurant, or you could hear someone doing something, for example, booking a holiday.

You have 10 seconds to read the question. Then you listen to the recording and choose the correct answer for the question (**A**, **B** or **C**). The questions are often *wh-* questions, like *What activity is she describing?* There is one example to show you how to answer the questions.

Section 2

Section 2 of the written paper tests how well you can understand information you hear. You show this understanding when you write all of the words you hear. You will also need to check your spelling.

In Section 2 you listen to a short recording and write down the words you hear. First, you listen to the whole recording and don't write anything. Then you listen to the recording again with some pauses in it. Write down the words you hear, while you are listening or when you hear the pause. There is no example.

Section 3

Section 3 of the written paper tests how well you can listen for the information that you need in longer recordings like a message, an announcement, or a conversation. You will also need to check your spelling.

You listen to two recordings with one or two speakers asking for or giving information. The information you hear will be simple facts. You then use what you hear to write the missing words in a text or notes. There is one text or set of notes for each recording. You complete five gaps for each recording, so there are ten gaps to complete in total. You have time to read the notes before you listen to each recording and you hear each recording twice. You should write the missing words while you're listening to the recording.

Go to the **Grammar Bank** on pages 136–149 for reference and extra practice.

Go to **Vocabulary maps** on **Pearson English Portal** for useful language.

Do **Vocabulary activities** on **Pearson Practice English** app for more practice.

HOW TO DO SECTION 1

What does Section 1 test?

Section 1 tests your listening skills. It tests how well you can understand simple information and conversations about everyday topics and simple instructions. You could hear descriptions, instructions, announcements (people saying information to a group of people, e.g. at a train station) or listen to a conversation.

> **In this section, you are being tested on:**
> **Your general listening skills**
> - If you can understand people when they speak clearly and slowly.
> - If you can understand the simple information you need in your daily life.
>
> **Your understanding of announcements and instructions**
> - If you can understand the most important information in short, clear, simple messages and announcements.
> - If you can understand simple directions and instructions.
>
> **Your understanding of conversations between native speakers**
> - If you can understand where the speakers are, who the speakers are, and what the speakers are talking about.

How to do Section 1

- Read the example question at the start of the section. Then listen to the recording and find the answer to the question. Use the example to check how to show your options (you mark the box for the correct answer: **A**, **B** or **C**).
- You only hear each recording once. Read the question and look at the pictures in the 10 seconds you have before you listen. Underline important words in the question.
- Think carefully about what you can see in the pictures, and what language you need to describe each one. Then listen for this language in the recording.
- Remember that you will hear information about more than one of the pictures in the recording. You need to listen carefully to make sure the picture you choose gives the answer to the question.
- If you aren't sure what the correct answer is, decide if any options are clearly wrong and then look at the other answers and try to answer every question.
- Think about what kind of information *wh* words in questions ask you to look for and practice answering different kinds of questions. In Section 1, the questions often begin with a *wh-* word, which helps you understand what information you need to find. Underline and remember the *wh-* word for each question and then listen for the type of information it asks for.
- To prepare for this section of the exam, try to listen to native speakers (people from a country where English is the main language). While you are listening, think about where the speakers are and who the speakers are. Try to notice the most important information they talk about.

Scoring

> In Section 1, there is a total of 10 points. You get 1 point for each correct answer and 0 points for an incorrect answer.

SECTION 1: TRAINING

Focus on the instructions

1 Read the Section 1 instructions and look at the tasks on pages 11–13.

    a How many questions are there?

    b How many possible answers are there for each question?

    c How much time do you have to read each question before you listen?

    d How much time do you have to choose the correct answer?

Focus on the questions

1 Look at question 1 on page 11. What information will help you know which classroom it is?

2 In question 2, what information do you need about the boy's bag?

3 In question 3, how many of the clothes do you think the man will talk about? Does he talk about all three pictures? How do you know which one is the answer?

4 In question 4, what do you usually book through the phone?

5 In question 5, look at the pictures of the three jobs. What are the jobs? What other words do you think you could hear for each picture to help you find the answer? Think about the places in the pictures.

6 In question 6, how many buses do you hear about? What do they say about the *first* bus?

7 In question 7, do you need to listen for:

    a something that happened in the past?

    b something that is happening now?

    c something that will happen in the future?

8 In question 8, which of the words in the box do you think you'll hear in the conversation? Are there any other words you think you'll hear too?

> eggs   pay   plate   potatoes   waiter

9 In question 9, what do you need to understand so you can choose the correct answer?

    a a description of a town

    b directions to a place

    c information about a hotel

10 In question 10, describe the people you can see in each picture. How many are there? Are they men, women, girls or boys?

Focus on the language

1 Choose the correct words to complete the sentences from the recordings for Section 1 in Test 1.

    a Please *bring / come* to G34, which is opposite G28, the big art room.

    b On the shelf *above / on* the seat.

    c It's actually *over / too* short for me.

    d Could we have a *bed / table* by the window – to sit and look at the sea?

    e I'm happy I don't work *in / on* the kitchen.

    f Buses go from the bus station to Westside every twenty minutes …. So, they *start / leave* at ten, ten twenty and so on.

    g They're moving *into / out* of the city to a piece of land by the airport.

    h Today, it's *been / got* cream, fish and some vegetables in it.

    i Walk up Park Street, and go *under / past* some shops on your right.

    j So, there'll be just *four / three* of us – two against one!

2 ▶ Listen to the recordings for Section 1 and complete tasks 1–10.

TEST I

Section I

Questions 1–10

▶ You have 10 seconds to read each question. Listen and put a cross ☒ in the box next to the correct answer, as in the example. You have 10 seconds to choose the correct option.

Example What activity is she describing?

A ☒   B ☐   C ☐

---

1   Which classroom will the lesson be in next week?

A ☐   B ☐   C ☐

---

2   Where did the boy leave his bag?

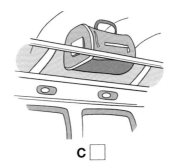

A ☐   B ☐   C ☐

Section I

3   What does the man want to change?

      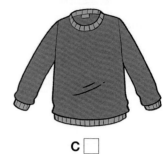

A ☐   B ☐   C ☐

4   What is the woman booking?

A ☐   B ☐   C ☐

5   What is the man's new job?

   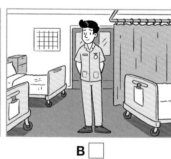   

A ☐   B ☐   C ☐

6   What time is the first bus to Westside each day?

A ☐   B ☐   C ☐

7 Where will Harrison's factory move to?

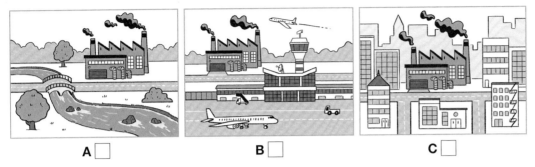

A ☐ B ☐ C ☐

8 What is in the dish that the waiter describes?

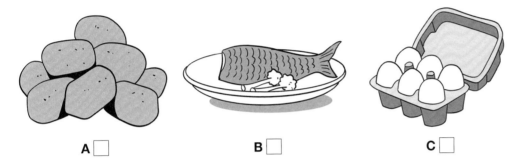

A ☐ B ☐ C ☐

9 Where is Newgate Hotel?

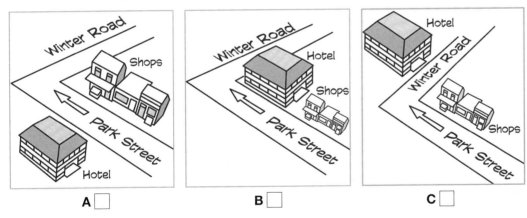

A ☐ B ☐ C ☐

10 Who is going to play tennis tonight?

A ☐ B ☐ C ☐

HOW TO DO SECTION 2

What does Section 2 test?

Section 2 tests your listening and writing skills. You need to understand a recording and then write all of the sentences you hear. You also need to spell the words in your sentences correctly. The recording you hear could be instructions, a news report, announcements or information. The recordings usually describe something and use more formal words than in Section 1.

> **In this section, you are being tested on:**
> **Your general listening skills**
> • If you can understand people when they speak clearly and slowly.
> • If you can understand a sentence and write it correctly.
> **Your general writing skills**
> • If you can write simple phrases and sentences.
> • If you can spell words correctly.

How to do Section 2

> • Read the instructions and underline the topic that the speaker will talk about. Think about the words you could hear when someone is talking about this topic before you listen.
> • Don't write anything the first time you listen to the recording. Try to understand what the speaker wants to say and notice the most important words he or she says. The speaker will usually make the most important words sound stronger.
> • The second time you listen to the recording, write the words you hear when you hear them. Leave a space between words if you don't understand one that you hear. When there's a pause in the recording, look at the spaces between the words and think about what the missing words could be. Use what you know about the subject and about vocabulary and grammar to help you do this.
> • There could be some words you didn't write down or aren't sure about. Read the whole sentence and think about what word or words could go in those empty gaps.
> • Read your notes and check that your sentences are clear and that your spelling is correct. Look for words that are easy to spell wrong, like *too/to, their/there*.
> • Try to improve your grammar before the test. This will help you to put the correct words in the spaces in your sentences. Also try to improve your spelling. To help you do this, look at longer words or words that are easy to spell wrong. Try looking at a word and then, without looking again, write it a few times on a piece of paper. Then look at the word again to check if you spelled it correctly.

Scoring

> In Section 2, there is a total of 10 points. You get 1 point for each correct answer and 0 points for an incorrect answer.

SECTION 2: TRAINING

Focus on the instructions

1 Read the Section 2 task instructions on page 16.

   a How many times will you hear the recording?

   b What shouldn't you do the first time you listen?

   c What's different about the recording the second time you listen?

   d What do you do the second time you hear the recording?

   e What do you need to check when you finish writing?

Focus on the questions

1 When you go to the cinema, what information do you usually get? Complete the sentences with the correct words.

   a _____ the film starts.

   b _____ cinema the film will be in.

   c _____ you can go into the cinema and find your seat.

   d What you need to do with your mobile phone – turn it _____.

2 Which words do you think you could hear in an announcement at the cinema? Choose the words in the box and then think of more words, if you can.

> book film lunch phone start table
> ticket turn off turn on

3 What do you think you will hear in the announcement? You can choose more than one answer.

   a Information about the film.

   b Information about the cinema.

   c Instructions for the people who are going to watch the film.

   d Questions for the people who are going to watch the film.

   e Something friendly to welcome the people to the cinema.

Focus on the language

1 Complete these sentences with your own words. You will hear these sentences in the recording.

The film _____ start _____ five minutes. _____ find your seats now. If _____ have _____ phone, turn it _____. We hope you _____ the film.

2 ▶ Listen to the recording for Section 2 and check your answers.

3 ▶ Read the sentences again. Where does the speaker pause in the recording? Listen again and write // in the places where the speaker pauses.

4 Read the text. Find five spelling mistakes. Rewrite the text using the correct words.

Hello and welcome to the show. Their are some interesting people on the show today.

_____

_____

We will talk about how to save money when you're shoping online. Than we will talk about beutiful

_____

_____

Norway and hear more about places to visit there to.

_____

_____

Section 2

Question 11

▶ You will hear a recording about watching a film at a cinema. Listen to the whole recording once. Then you will hear the recording again with pauses for you to write down what you hear. Make sure you spell the words correctly.

HOW TO DO SECTION 3

What does Section 3 test?

Section 3 tests your listening skills and how well you can listen for facts, or missing information from notes or sentences. This could be names, dates and times, and other information. The two recordings you hear in this section could be conversations between someone who wants to do something and someone who is helping them (e.g. one person wants to take part in an English course, and the other person has some information about the course). You could also hear announcements or phone messages.

In this section, you are being tested on:

Your general listening skills

- If you can understand people who speak clearly and slowly.
- If you can understand the simple information you need in your daily life.
- If you can understand phrases you hear when people are talking about things from daily life.

Your understanding of recordings from real-life situations

- If you can understand the most important information in short, simple recordings about general topics.

How to do Section 3

- Read the texts with the missing words before you listen to the recording. Look at the words that come before and after the gap.
- Try to decide which words, or which types of information, could fill the gap before you listen. For example, could it be a name, a time, a number, part of a telephone number?
- If it isn't clear exactly what information should go in the gap, think about what type of word it could be. For example, if the word before the gap is *a, an* or *the*, you know that the missing word is a noun. You could write *n* or *noun* near the gap to help you when you are listening.
- Look at the words that give the most important information in the sentence. These will usually be nouns or verbs. Use them to help you understand what the sentence is about. Underline these words and look at them while you're listening.
- After you've listened, read the notes again with your answer words in them. Check if your answers are right for the sentences and check your spelling.
- Make sure you fill all the spaces. If you aren't sure which word to write in a space, write any word that is possible in the sentence.
- To prepare for the exam, practise listening to recordings of different real-life situations and try to understand the most important information in them. You could write this information down.

Scoring

In Section 3, there is a total of 10 points. You get 1 point for each correct answer and 0 points for an incorrect answer.

SECTION 3: TRAINING

Focus on the instructions

1 Read the instructions for the Section 3 tasks on pages 19–20.

  a How many gaps are there in each task?

  b What do you listen to in the first task (questions 12–16)?

  c What do you listen to in the second task (questions 17–21)?

  d How many times will you hear each recording?

Focus on the questions

1 Look at question 12. What kind of word do you need to use before a month?

  a a number

  b a day

  c a preposition

2 In question 13, what information do you need to write in the gap?

3 In question 14, what type of information do you need to write in the gap?

  a a number

  b a name

  c a date

4 In question 15, what skills can you practise in a language course?

5 In question 16, what type of information do you need to write in the gap?

  a a number

  b a name

  c a date

6 In question 17, the word *on* can come before

  a a time (e.g. *6 a.m*).

  b a day of the week.

  c a place name.

7 In question 18, what does *p.m.* always come after?

8 In question 20, which words fit best in the gap? Think about grammar. More than one answer is correct.

  a foot

  b car

  c boat

  d train

9 In question 21, what type of information do you need to write in the gap?

  a a number

  b a name

  c a time

Focus on the language

1 Choose the correct words to complete the sentences. All the sentences come from the recordings from questions 12–16 on page 19.

  a At World Language School, we have places left for our next courses, which start *at / on* the 19*nd / th* of September.

  b We now offer classes *for / over* beginner to advanced students in five languages.

  c ... and for the *first / next* time this year, we're giving French classes.

  d Each course has two terms, and is 25 weeks *along / long*.

  e Our classes are small – no *less / more* than 15 students per class.

  f During the course, some lessons are for listening, some for writing and some for reading. But every lesson also includes a *science/speaking* exercise.

2 ▶ Listen to the recordings for Section 3 in Test 1 to check your answers and complete the Section 3 task, questions 17–21.

Section 3

Questions 12–16

▶ You will hear an advertisement on the radio. First, read the notes below. Then listen and complete the notes with information from the advertisement. You will hear the recording twice.

Example Name of school: ....World............ Language School

12 Date next courses start: .... September

13 New language offered this year: ....

14 How long the courses are: .... weeks

15 All lessons have: .... practice

16 Name of person to contact: Suzanne ....

Section 3

Questions 17–21

▶ You will hear a woman asking for information from a boat travel company. First, read the notes below. Then listen and complete the notes with information from the conversation. You will hear the recording twice.

Example The woman wants information about a boat that's going to ....*Liverpool*........ .

17 The woman is travelling at 9:30 on .... evening next week.

18 The woman can check in from .... p.m. until 8:30 p.m.

19 The telephone number to ring if the weather is bad is 0843 ....

20 The woman is travelling from her home by ....

21 It will take her .... minutes to walk to the boat.

OVERVIEW: READING

About the Reading sections

The Reading sections are part of the written test which is 1 hour 35 minutes long at A2 level. There are four Reading sections in the written test, which are Sections 4–7. Each section is different. You will read short texts that describe things or give directions and instructions. You will also read other texts, including emails, letters or articles.

Section 4

Section 4 tests how well you can understand the main idea in a text and also specific information in a text.

You read five short texts. Each has a gap. There are three possible answers for each gap (**A**, **B** or **C**). You must choose the correct word or phrase for the gap. The texts can be labels (texts on things that you buy, like food), instructions, signs (texts that you see when you're travelling or walking around), notices (texts that give you information), menus, advertisements (texts that tell you to buy something) or announcements (information given to a group of people about something that's happening or is going to happen). There is one example to show you how to answer the questions.

Section 5

Section 5 of the written paper tests how well you can understand details in texts.

You read a short text and answer a question about it. The answer to the question is one of three pictures under the text. You choose the correct picture (**A**, **B** or **C**). The texts you read will, for example, describe something or give directions to a place. When you read the texts, you need to understand what this thing or place is. There is one example to show you how to answer the questions.

Section 6

Section 6 of the written paper tests how well you can understand the main ideas in texts.

You read two texts and answer four questions about each text. When you answer the questions, you should write phrases, not full sentences. The texts you read could be letters, emails, magazine articles or information about events or things you can buy. The questions you answer will often be *wh*-questions that test your understanding of the information in the text. There is one example to show you how to answer the questions.

Section 7

Section 7 tests how well you can find and understand detailed information in a text.

You read a longer text in Section 7. Then you use information in the text to write missing words in some notes. The missing information will be one one to three words. The text you read could be a letter, an email, an advertisement, a newspaper article, a magazine article or information from a website. There is one example to show you how to answer the questions.

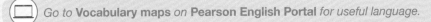
Go to the **Grammar Bank** *on pages 136–149 for reference and extra practice.*

Go to **Vocabulary maps** *on* **Pearson English Portal** *for useful language.*

Do **Vocabulary activities** *on* **Pearson Practice English** *app for more practice.*

HOW TO DO SECTION 4

What does Section 4 test?

Section 4 tests your reading skills and how well you can understand the main idea in a text. The texts you read in this section could be labels, instructions, signs, notices, menus, or advertisements. They could also be short notes, emails, semi-formal letters and announcements.

In this section, you are being tested on:

Your general reading skills

- If you can understand short, simple texts on general topics with simple, everyday language and vocabulary.

Your understanding of the main idea in a text

- If you can find the information you need in simple everyday texts like advertisements, menus, recipes and timetables.
- If you can find the information you need in lists (e.g. lists of people who do different jobs and their telephone numbers).
- If you can understand signs and notices (e.g. at the railway station; in a restaurant; or at work).

Your understanding of information in a text

- If you can find the information you need in simple texts like letters and short newspaper articles.

How to do Section 4

- First read the text and don't think about which words could go in the gaps. Try to get a general understanding of the text.
- Only one of the three words or phrases (**A**, **B** or **C**) which can go in the gap. Read the sentence and use the words before or after the gap to decide what type of word could go in it. Can it be a noun, a verb or an adjective? You could write *n* or *noun* for a noun near the gap to help you when you're reading the text.
- Look for links between the other words in the sentence and the three words you can choose. For example, if the sentence has the word *knife* in it, you can see a link between *knife* and *cut*.
- If you're not sure which answer is correct, decide which word or phrase you know is wrong and then look carefully at the others. Use the information in the text to help you choose one.
- If you still don't know the correct answer, it's better to choose any answer that's possible. Remember to give an answer for every question.
- Choose your answer for each gap and then read all of the sentences again to check if each one sounds correct.

Scoring

In Section 4, there is a total of 5 points. You get 1 point for each correct answer and 0 points for an incorrect answer.

SECTION 4: TRAINING

Focus on the instructions

1 Read the Section 4 instructions and look at the tasks on pages 24–25.

  a How many texts do you read?

  b What do you write next to the correct answer?

  c How many possible answers are there for each gap?

  d How many answers can you choose for each gap?

Focus on the questions

1 Look at questions 22–26 on pages 24–25. Which text (or texts) is:

  a a notice?

  b a recipe?

  c an advertisement?

2 What do all of the texts give the reader?

  a good news

  b instructions

  c information

3 Read the text from question 24. Where can you find a text like this?

4 What does the text from question 24 say?

  a Hotel guests can buy tickets for a city tour.

  b Hotel guests can go on a free city tour.

  c Hotel guests can walk around the city.

5 Read the text from question 24 again and choose the missing phrase for the gap.

  a come back

  b carry on

  c check in

6 The correct answer to question 24 means:

  a to arrive and get your key.

  b to return to a place.

  c to continue doing something.

7 Match the incorrect phrases from **5** with their definitions from **6**.

Focus on the language

1 Look at question 22. What does the text tell you?

  a How to cut vegetables.

  b How to cook fish and vegetables.

  c How to choose the right fish.

2 The correct answer for question 22 is *Cut*. Underline the word in the text that tells you this is the correct answer.

3 Why are the other two answers in question 22 wrong?

4 Look at question 25. What does the notice say?

  a An arts centre needs new actors.

  b An arts centre needs more money.

  c An arts centre needs new ideas.

5 The correct answer for question 25 is *show*. Underline the word in the text that tells you this is the correct answer.

6 Why are the other two answers in question 25 wrong?

Section 4

Questions 22–26

Read each text and put a cross ⊠ by the missing word or phrase, as in the example.

Example

Summerhill Theatre Club presents
'Romeo and Juliet'

Fri 15th June

Tickets £15 or £12 if you .... online.

A ⊠ buy

B ☐ make

C ☐ take

22

Put oil and salt on the fish.

.... up the vegetables with a knife.

Cook the fish and vegetables together for 12 minutes.

A ☐ Cut

B ☐ Wash

C ☐ Mix

23

Parkview Restaurant

Come to Parkview for great food at low prices.

15% off for groups of ten or more – join us for your next .... !

A ☐ service

B ☐ party

C ☐ bill

Section 4

24

Free Tour for Hotel Guests

See the city with us on foot!
We meet here at 10.00 and .... at 11.30.
Wear comfortable shoes!

A ☐ come back

B ☐ carry on

C ☐ check in

25

 Wanted: New Stars!

Fordham Arts Centre is looking for child actors for its new
.... in June.

Call Jill Woodson for more information: 0753 986758.

A ☐ painting club

B ☐ band

C ☐ show

26

Important notice!

Students must return all books before the end of .... because the school will be closed during the holiday.

A ☐ exam

B ☐ term

C ☐ library

HOW TO DO SECTION 5

What does Section 5 test?

Section 5 tests your reading skills and how well you can understand details in texts. You make a link between the details in a text and what you can see in a picture.

In this section, you are being tested on:

Your general reading skills

- If you can understand short, simple texts on general topics with simple, everyday language and vocabulary.

Your understanding of the main idea in a text

- If you can find the information you need in simple everyday texts like advertisements, menus, lists and timetables.
- If you can find the information you need in lists (e.g. shopping lists or a list of things to take on holiday).
- If you can understand signs and notices (e.g. at the railway station; in a restaurant; or at work).

Your understanding of instructions

- If you can understand simple instructions for daily activities.

Your understanding of information in a text

- If you can find all the information you need in simple texts like letters and short newspaper articles.

Your understanding of emails and letters

- If you can understand short, simple letters and emails on everyday topics.

How to do Section 5

- First read the whole text quickly and try to get a general understanding of the text.
- Next, read the questions. Underline the words in the questions that tell you which information you need to find (e.g. _What food_ does the writer eat _before_ he does _exercise?_).
- Read the text again. Look for the information you underlined (e.g. _What food_ and the other words you underlined or words that have a similar meaning).
- When you find the correct information, look at the pictures. Choose the picture that shows you the correct information, or that matches your understanding.
- If you're not sure which answer is correct, decide which picture you know is wrong and then look at the others. What information is there in the text which can help you to choose the correct one?
- If you still don't know the correct answer, it's better to choose any answer that's possible. Remember to give an answer for every question.
- Read the question and the whole text again and check to see that you chose the correct picture.

Scoring

In Section 5, there is a total of 5 points. You get 1 point for each correct answer and 0 points for an incorrect answer.

SECTION 5: TRAINING

Focus on the instructions

1 Read the Section 5 instructions and look at the tasks on pages 28–30.

  a How many questions do you answer?

  b What do you write next to the correct picture?

  c How many pictures are there for each question?

  d Is there an example to show you how to answer?

Focus on the questions

1 Look at the questions 27–31.

  a Look at the example. You need to find information about:

    i a person.

    ii a place.

    iii a time.

  b Look at the pictures in the example. What can you see in each picture?

  c Read the text for the example question. How many of the places in the pictures are in the text?

  d The incorrect answers are *the park* and *the cinema*. Why does Ali talk about them?

  e Look at question 27. What type of text is it?

    i an email

    ii a notice

    iii a blog post

  f Read question 27 carefully. What are you looking for in the text?

    i Something the writer eats after he goes running.

    ii Something other people usually eat.

    iii Something the writer eats before exercising.

  g Read the text for question 27 and look at the pictures. Which food is an incorrect answer because the writer doesn't eat it?

    i vegetables

    ii chicken

  h Now you have two answers to choose from, **b** and **c**. Which one is incorrect? Why?

Focus on the language

1 Look at the questions 27–31. Read the text for question 28. Underline the words that give the most important information in the text.

> **Student information**
>
> Classes start next week! Remember to get your college ID card from the Student Office this week. You'll need it to use the library during the course. Don't forget the welcome party next week! It'll be fun!

2 Read question 28 and underline the words that tell you: *What must students do before the course begins?*

3 What other information does the text include? More than one answer is correct.

  a What they must do during the course.

  b What they must do after the course

  c What they can do next week.

4 When will students need to use the library?

  a before the course

  b during the course

  c after the course

5 When is the welcome party?

  a this week

  b next week

6 Choose the correct answer for question 28.

Section 5

Questions 27–31

For each question, put a cross ☒ in the box below the correct picture, as in the example.

Example

> Sarah,
>
> Let's eat at the restaurant opposite the park before the film. It's near the cinema so we'll have enough time. See you there!
>
> Ali

Where does Ali want to meet Sarah this evening?

A ☒   B ☐   C ☐

27 What food does the writer eat before he does exercise?

> ### My exercise plan
>
> It's important to eat before running. Some people eat vegetables, but I usually have one or two bananas because I think they give me more energy. After exercising, I always have chicken because it helps me build muscles.

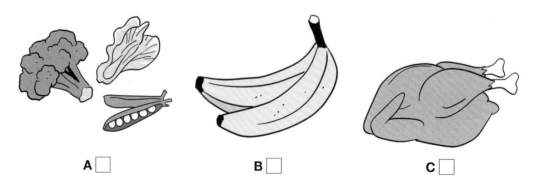

A ☐   B ☐   C ☐

Section 5

28   What must students do before the course begins?

> ### Student information
>
> Classes start next week! Remember to get your college ID card from the Student Office this week. You'll need it to use the library during the course. Don't forget the welcome party next week! It'll be fun!

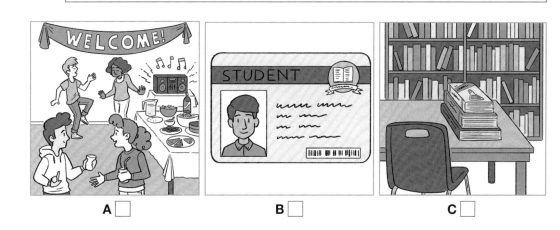

A ☐   B ☐   C ☐

29   Which of Tom's photos does Pete have a problem with?

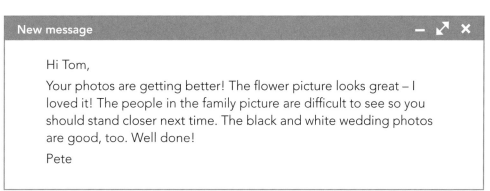

Hi Tom,

Your photos are getting better! The flower picture looks great – I loved it! The people in the family picture are difficult to see so you should stand closer next time. The black and white wedding photos are good, too. Well done!

Pete

A ☐   B ☐   C ☐

Section 5

30 What is the correct picture for the children's event?

> **City Events**
>
> International Music Festival. Music from all around the world.
>
> 19.00–02.00, Concert Hall, 19 June, Over-18s.
>
> Tickets £20
>
> **Cooking Club (adults only). Learn to cook at Bilson Hall!**
>
> 19 June, 09.00–14.00, £25 per class
>
> **Carson Park Football Competition. Open to players under ten years old.**
>
> £10 per team. 30 June.

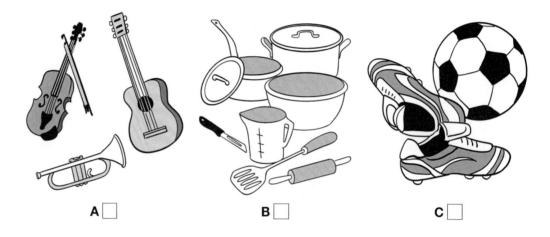

A ☐   B ☐   C ☐

31 What do students need for the school trip?

> **Class trip**
>
> Our school trip will be great fun but remember to bring a coat because the weather changes quickly. Don't bring any cash with you – you will be given lunch after visiting the national park. And please wear walking boots!

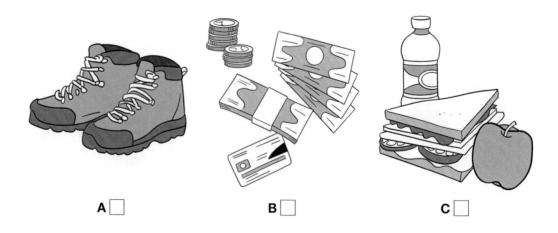

A ☐   B ☐   C ☐

HOW TO DO SECTION 6

What does Section 6 test?

Section 6 tests your reading skills and how well you can understand information in a text. The texts you read could be letters, emails, magazine articles, or information about things you can buy or events.

In this section, you are being tested on:

Your general reading skills
- If you can understand short, simple texts on general topics with simple, everyday language and vocabulary.

Your understanding of instructions
- If you can understand simple instructions for daily activities (e.g. a public telephone).

Your understanding of information in a text
- If you can find all the information you need in simple texts like emails, letters and short articles.

Your understanding of emails and letters
- If you can understand short, simple letters and emails on everyday topics.

How to do Section 6

- First read the whole text quickly and try to get a general understanding of the text.
- Read the example question and answer. Find the answer in the text. The answer is always a short phrase, not a complete sentence.
- Then read the questions. Underline the *wh-* question word at the start of the question or any other important words in the question.
- Read the text again. Which words did you underline? Where they people, places or times?
- You will find the answer to the example question at the start of the text. The answer to the next question comes next in the text and the answer to the third question after that.
- Remember that there is always some information in the text that you don't need. Make sure that you use exactly the information you need and nothing more.
- Read the whole text again when you've written your answers. Check that you've found the correct information.
- If you're not sure about the answer to the question, write a possible answer. For example, if the question asks you to find a place, write any name of a place that's in the text.

Scoring

In Section 6, there is a total of 8 points. You get 1 point for each correct answer and 0 points for an incorrect answer.

SECTION 6: TRAINING

Focus on the instructions

1 Read the Section 6 instructions and look at the tasks.

a What type of text do you read in the first task?

b What type of text do you read in the second task?

c How many questions do you answer for each text?

d Do you have answers to choose from or do you write the answers?

Focus on the questions

1 Look at the first task in Section 6 on page 33.

a What type of information do you need to answer question 32?

b What information do you need to answer question 33?

c For question 34, what are the two films that are named in the text?

d In question 35, which film do you need to find information about?

2 Look at the second task in Section 6 on page 34.

a In question 36, which camping trip do you need to find information about?

b In question 37, which people do you need to find information about?

c What type of information do you need to answer question 38?

   i a time

   ii a place

   iii a reason

d In question 39, which tent do you need to find information about?

Focus on the language

1 Look at questions 32–35 on page 33.

a i When can Lucy not go to the cinema? Why?

   ii When can Lucy go to the cinema?

b Underline the words in the text that tell you that the *Odeon* is cheaper.

c Underline the word that tells you Mary has seen *Box 2* before.

d Which positive adjective does Lucy use for Tommy Jones' last film? What does this adjective describe?

2 Look at questions 36–39 on page 34.

a Underline the words that tell you the writer is writing about her first camping holiday.

b Underline the word that tells you that the writer's children enjoy doing something.

c In the sentence, *I think it's the fresh air*, 'it' is

   i the tent the writer uses on camping holidays.

   ii the reason the writer sleeps well on camping holidays.

   iii the reason why her children love cooking.

d Underline the words that tell you how many people can sleep in the writer's new tent.

Questions 32–35

Read the email below and answer the questions.

New message   – ⤢ ✕

Hi Mary,

I can't come to the cinema with you on Friday because it's my brother's birthday party. Shall we go on Wednesday? Let's go to the Odeon, not the Cineplex, because there's 25 percent off with your college card.

Which film shall we see? You've already seen *Box 2*, and I'm not interested in *Dark House*. We could watch the new Tommy Jones film. People say it's funny. His last film was really sad but the music was beautiful.

Lucy

Example Who is having a party?

.... *Lucy's brother* ....

32   When does Lucy want to see Mary?

....

33   Which cinema has cheaper tickets for students?

....

34   Which film has Mary watched before?

....

35   What did Lucy like about Tommy Jones' last film?

....

Section 6

Questions 36–39

Read the magazine article below and answer the questions.

Go Camping!

Forget staying in a hotel or going to an expensive beach club, and try camping instead. I went camping for the first time ten years ago with some friends, and now I go every year with my family.

We walk in the mountains and swim in rivers. The children love cooking food outside! I always sleep well on camping holidays. I think it's the fresh air. We've just bought a six-person tent, which I can't wait to use!

Example Which holiday costs a lot of money?

.... *beach club* ....

---

36 Who did the writer go with on her first camping holiday?

....

37 What do the writer's children enjoy doing?

....

38 Why does the writer sleep a lot when she goes camping?

....

39 How many people can sleep in the writer's new tent?

....

HOW TO DO SECTION 7

What does Section 7 test?

Section 7 tests your reading skills and how well you can find details in a text. You read a longer text of around 100–150 words. Then you use the information in this text to complete gaps in some notes. The missing information will be one to three words. The text you read could be a letter, an email, information about events or things you can buy articles, websites or textbooks.

> **In this section, you are being tested on:**
> **Your general reading skills**
> - If you can understand short, simple texts on general topics with simple, everyday language and vocabulary.
> **Your understanding of information in a text**
> - If you can find the information you need in simple texts like emails, letters and short articles.

How to do Section 7

- First read the whole text quickly. Don't look at the notes. Try to get a general understanding of the text.
- Then read questions 40–46 and underline the most important word or words in each one. For example, in question 40, the most important words are *oldest age*.
- Look at the example question and find the answer in the text. The answer to question 40 will always come after this in the text. Look at how the answer is written – it's a word or phrase, and not a full sentence.
- Read the text again. Look for the information you underlined in the first question. Maybe you'll need to look for an example of this information or words that have a similar meaning.
- Find the answer to the first question. Then look at the example answer and write your answer in the same way. You will see that you don't need to write more than three words in your answers.
- Repeat the process above for all of the other questions.
- Answer all the questions, even if you aren't sure what the correct answer is. Choose a word or words which are the type of information you need or which have a similar meaning to the words you underlined.
- When you've answered all the questions, check your answers. Look for your answers in the text and check what information they're giving. Is this the information you need to answer the questions?
- Always write an answer for every question, even if you're not sure.
- Remember to spell the words you write correctly and use capital letters for words like countries and names.

Scoring

In Section 7, there is a total of 7 points. You get 1 point for each correct answer and 0 points for an incorrect answer.

SECTION 7: TRAINING

Focus on the instructions

1 Read the Section 7 instructions and look at the task on page 37.

    a What type of text do you read in this task?

    b What do you need to complete?

    c How many gaps are there?

    d How many words can you write in each gap?

Focus on the questions

1 Look at the example question on page 37. Where in the text will you find the information you need?

    a the beginning of the text

    b the middle of the text

    c the end of the text

2 For question 40, what does number *13* tell you?

    a the youngest age you can enter

    b the oldest age you can enter

3 For question 41, which country or countries can you find in the text?

4 Look at question 42. There are three dates in the text. Match each date to the correct description.

    a 31 May   first date to perform in the competition

    b 30 June   last date to perform in the competition

    c 31 July   last date to join the competition

5 In question 43, what information about the programme do you need to find?

6 In question 44, what kind of prize can you win in this competition?

7 In question 45, where in the text can you find useful information about the types of song people can sing?

    a the beginning of the text

    b the middle of the text

    c the end of the text

8 In question 46, what type of information will be in your answer?

    a a name

    b a date

    c a number

Focus on the language

1 Read the first sentence of the text. What phrase tells you the youngest and oldest ages that you can enter the competition?

2 In the second sentence, the word *across* tells you that you can take part in the competition:

    a In one place in Canada.

    b In every place in Canada.

    c In places all around Canada.

3 Which words before a date in the text tell you that this is the latest date for doing something?

4 Which adjective in the text tells you what kind of programme *Be a Star* is?

    a further

    b national

    c interesting

5 Which words in the text tell you the type of song you can sing?

6 Which word in the text means the money you pay to do something?

Questions 40–46

Read the advertisement for a competition and complete the notes. Write **no more than three words** from the advertisement in each gap.

Be a Star singing competition

Be a Star is an exciting new singing competition for young people who are 13 to 18!

If you love to sing and want to be a star one day, then sing at one of the *Be a Star* events across Canada this summer. These will be in Vancouver, Calgary, Toronto and Montreal.

Sounds interesting? Then go to the *Be a Star* website to complete the form no later than 31 May. From 30 June to 31 July, we are going to watch thousands of teenagers performing, so we can choose 25 singers to compete on the *Be a Star* TV show. These lucky teens will sing on national television this September to try and win cash prizes for first, second and third place!

Sing any pop or rock song.

The entry fee is $15 per person or $35 per group.

For further information, please contact Laura Duchamp on email laura@beastar.com

---

Example Name of the competition: .... *Be a Star* ....

40   The oldest age you can enter the competition:

....

41   The country where you can take part: ....

42   The latest date you can join: ....

43   The programme will be on TV in: ....

44   Three people will receive: ....

45   The types of songs you can sing: ....

46   The cost for a band to enter: ....

OVERVIEW: WRITING

About the Writing sections

The Writing sections are part of the written test which is 1 hour 35 minutes long at A2 level. There are two Writing sections, which are Sections 8 and 9. Each section is different.

In Section 8, you will write a short text which is an example of correspondence. Correspondence is the activity of writing to communicate with other people and that could be in an email, a letter, a note, a postcard or a blog entry. You will use information from the article you read in Section 7 of the Reading section to write your text. For example, you could write an email to a friend to ask them to do an activity from the article in Section 7.

In Section 9, you will look at three pictures and use what you see to write a short text about them. In your text, you will either describe what is happening in the pictures or write a story about what you can see in the pictures.

Section 8

Section 8 shows the examiner if you can write simple sentences to give information in everyday situations; use simple grammar and vocabulary; use words like *and*, *but* and *because*; and use correct spelling. Your text also needs to have the correct organisation for an email, a letter, a postcard, a note or a blog entry. This should include a good opening and closing part, with 3–4 main things included in the text.

You write a short text, which could be an email, a letter, a postcard, a note or a blog entry. You can use the information you read in Section 7 in this text.

You have three things to include in your text, like saying why you want to do something, giving some information, or asking a question. You need to write between 50 and 70 words.

Section 9

Section 9 shows the examiner if you can write simple sentences to give information in everyday situations; use simple grammar and vocabulary; use words like *and*, *but* and *because*; and use correct spelling. Your text also needs to describe what you can see or what is happening in all three pictures.

You write a description or a narrative (e.g. diary entry, blog post, short story) based on what is happening in three pictures. Together these three pictures tell a story of something that happened.

You can choose from two topics, e.g. music or camping, and there are three pictures for each topic. You read a sentence about the situation that the three pictures show. Then you look at the pictures and write a piece of text on what is happening in the pictures. You need to write between 80 and 100 words.

 *Go to the **Grammar Bank** on pages 136–149 for reference and extra practice.*

 *Go to the **Writing Bank** on pages 168–171 for useful language and practice.*

HOW TO DO SECTION 8

What does Section 8 test?

Section 8 tests your writing skills. The examiner wants to see how well you can write texts that give other people information (correspondence).

> **In this section, you are being tested on:**
> **Your general writing skills**
> - If you can write short and simple notes about things that are happening now or things you need now.
>
> **Writing emails and letters**
> - If you can write very simple personal letters saying *thank you* or saying *sorry*.

How to do Section 8

- If you write a more formal or official email or letter, you need to start it with *Dear Mr/Ms +* surname, and end it with a word or phrase, like *Regards* (email).
- If you write an informal email, an informal letter, a postcard or a note, you can use a more informal style. You can start your text with *Hi* or *Hello* and end it with *See you soon!* or *Thanks!*
- The question always tells you what kind of text to write and who you are writing to. Use this information to plan your answer.
- The question also gives you three points that you must include in your answer. Sometimes you need to think of your own ideas (e.g. 'Say why you want to sing in the competition'). Think about what you can say to answer each point. Think about interesting language you can use.
- If one of the points starts with a word like *ask, invite* or *suggest*, you must do this clearly in your letter or email. Think of a good phrase to ask, invite or suggest that you can use in your text.
- Remember that you can and should use information from Section 7 of the Reading section of the written test in your text. Take facts from the Section 7 text and write them in your own words if possible. Don't copy too many words or whole sentences from the Section 7 text.
- You should use simple vocabulary for everyday things, people and activities in your text. You should also use different grammar structures (e.g. The present simple, present continuous and past simple). Remember that your text doesn't need to be perfect, but you should always check your text carefully for mistakes when you've finished writing it.
- You need to use linking words, like *and, but* and *because* in your text to go from one idea to the next, instead of writing a list of different ideas.
- You should write between 50 and 70 words, but it's OK to only write 44 words or to write up to 77 words.

Scoring

In Section 8, there is a total of 10 points. You will get points for how well you can give information in a short text like an email and how well you can use grammar and vocabulary.

SECTION 8: TRAINING

Focus on the instructions

1 Read the Section 8 instructions and look at the task on page 41.

    a Where do you get the information you need to write your text?

    b What type of text do you need to write?

    c Who are you writing to?

    d How many words do you need to write?

Focus on the questions

1 Look at the text in Section 7 on page 37 again.

    a What can you win if you enter the competition?

    b Which cities can you sing in?

    c Which contact information for Laura Duchamp is in the text?

2 Now look at Section 8 on page 41.

    a How many things do you need to include in your text?

    b What types of information do you need to give in your email? More than one answer is correct.

    i Ask a question.

    ii Say sorry for something.

    iii Give a reason.

    iv Explain something.

    v Describe something.

    c Put these things in the order you'll write them in your email.

    i a place

    ii a question about things

    iii a reason

Focus on the language

1 What would be the best way to start your text?

    a Hi Laura

    b Dear Laura

    c Good morning

2 Which phrase means *be in the competition*?

    a take off

    b take place

    c take part

3 Which word can you use to give a reason for joining the competition?

    a because

    b about

    c and

4 What's the best phrase to say which place you want to sing in the most? Check the question.

    a I'd prefer to ...

    b I really want to ...

    c I personally like ...

5 Which word can you use to say that this is your last sentence or question in your text?

    a firstly

    b after that

    c finally

6 Which question can you ask to find out what you need to bring?

    a What do people usually bring home with them?

    b Can you tell me about bringing something?

    c Do I need to bring anything with me?

7 What would be the best way to end your text?

    a thanks

    b bye

    c regards

SECTION 8 WRITING

Question 47

Use the information in **Section 7** to help you write your answer.

You have read about the singing competition on the *Be a Star* website. Now write an email to Laura Duchamp. Write **50–70 words** and include the following information:

- Say why you want to sing in the competition.
- Tell Laura which city you would prefer to sing in.
- Ask Laura what you need to bring.

HOW TO DO SECTION 9

What does Section 9 test?

Section 9 tests your writing skills. The examiner wants to see how well you can use three pictures to write a short story, a blog post or a diary entry.

In this section, you are being tested on:

Your general writing skills

- If you can use words like *and, but* and *because* to join one idea to another idea.

Your creative writing skills

- If you can write about everyday life, e.g. people, places, a job or study experience; and if you can join your sentences together.
- If you can write very short, basic descriptions of events, past activities and personal experiences.

How to do Section 9

- Look at the two topics and the three pictures for each one. Choose a topic that you find interesting and which you think you can write about.
- When you've chosen your topic, look very carefully at the three pictures for it. Describe what you can see or tell the story to yourself. Think about the language you will need.
- Remember to include all the details you can see in the pictures in your text. Go back to look at the pictures again while you're writing.
- If you write a diary entry, remember to use *I*, e.g. *I went to a concert last weekend.* Imagine that you had the experiences in the pictures. If the situation is that you did something with a friend, think of a name for that friend.
- If you write a short story or a description, you don't need to use *I*. Instead you can use *he, she, they* or the names of people.
- If you're writing a description, make your language as interesting as possible. Think about using interesting adjectives and verbs, or adverbs to describe how people move or act.
- As well as what people do, talk about how people feel in the story or description.
- Try to use different language structures and different vocabulary. If all your sentences start the same way (e.g. *There are two girls. There is a park. There is a band.*), your text will be quite boring. If you notice that you're using the same word a lot, try to think of another, more interesting word you can use.
- It's very important to use *and, but* and *because* to make links between ideas in your text in this section. The examiner will check if you have done that.
- When you have finished writing, read your text again and check it very carefully. Make sure you have written about everything in the pictures and that your story makes sense. Check your spelling, and any grammar that people often get wrong (e.g. single and plural verbs, prepositions).
- You should write between 80 and 100 words, but it's OK to only write 78 words or to write up to 110 words.

Scoring

In Section 9, there is a total of 10 points. You will get marks for how well you can communicate information in a short text like an email and how well you can use grammar and vocabulary.

SECTION 9: TRAINING

Focus on the instructions

1 Read the Section 9 instructions on page 44.

   a Where do you get the information about the details you need to include in your text?

   b How many words do you need to write?

Focus on the questions

1 Which two topics can you choose from?

2 Look at the sentence and the three pictures for topic A.

   a Who are the *two friends*? Decide who you will talk about.
     i you and one of your friends
     ii two of your friends
     iii the two people in the pictures

   b What type of text do you need to write?
     i an email
     ii a description
     iii a diary entry

   c What are the two friends doing in the pictures?
     i Going for a walk in the park.
     ii Going to see a band in the park.
     iii Playing a concert in the park.

3 Now answer the questions about topic B.

   a Who is Max?
     i a friend of yours
     ii someone you know
     iii someone you don't know

   b What did Max do last summer?
     i went camping
     ii went walking
     iii went skiing

   c How did Max feel about what he did last summer?
     i He enjoyed it.
     ii He didn't like it.
     iii He thought it was OK.

4 Which of these two topics would you prefer to write about? Why?

Focus on the language

1 Look at topic A again. Which tense do you need to use to describe the pictures?

   a the present continuous

   b the present simple

   c the past simple

2 Read the sentences from a model answer and complete them with the correct words:

They met _____ the main entrance _____ the park and bought the tickets. At first the weather was very sunny and the music was great _____ after a while it started to get cloudy.

3 Now look at topic B.

   a When exactly did the things in the pictures happen?
     i last summer
     ii this summer
     iii they're happening at the moment

   b What is the best way to start your story?
     i Max is really enjoying a camping trip with his family.
     ii Last summer, Max had a great time on a camping trip with his family.
     iii Max really enjoys camping trips with his family in the summer.

   c Read the sentence from a model answer. Which word can you use you between these two facts?

   Max drank some lemonade _____ his father drank some tea.

   d Complete this sentence from a model answer with the correct forms of the verbs in brackets.

   Max _____ (swim) in the lake and his parents _____ (relax) and _____ (watch) Max swimming.

Question 48

Choose **one** of the topics below and write your answer in **80–100 words**.

Either:

A Music

Last weekend two friends went to see a band in the park. Look at the pictures and write a description of what happened.

Or:

B Camping

Your friend Max had a great time camping with his family last summer. Look at the pictures and write a story about it.

Put a cross ☒ in the box next to the task you have chosen.

A ☐   B ☐

OVERVIEW: SPEAKING

About the Speaking sections

There are three Speaking sections in the test, which are Sections 10, 12 and 13. Each section is different, and you will either talk on your own or have a conversation with the examiner. In Section 10, you will answer questions about yourself from the examiner. In Section 12, the examiner gives you a picture. You describe what is happening in the picture and answer questions about it. In Section 13, you read a card with a situation on it and then take part in a role play based on the situation with the examiner. There is no Section 11 in the A2 level test.

Section 10 *1.5 minutes*

Section 10 opens the conversation at the start of the Speaking test and lets the examiner see how well you can talk about yourself and your everyday life.

The examiner will first ask you a short question about your everyday life or your opinions. You can give a short answer to this question. Then they will ask one or more questions to help you talk on your own for one minute. You should try to give longer answers to these questions.

Section 12 *2 minutes*

Section 12 shows the examiner how well you can use vocabulary and grammar to describe situations from everyday life.

The examiner will first give you a picture to look at. The picture will show a real-life situation, (e.g. a family walking in the forest with their dog). You take a quick look at the picture and then they will ask you to describe what you can see and what is happening in it (e.g. Where the people are, and what they are doing). You should talk for about a minute. If you talk for less than one minute and then stop, the examiner will ask you some extra questions about the picture so you keep talking for one whole minute. The examiner will then take the picture away from you.

Section 13 *1.5 minutes*

Section 13 shows the examiner how well you can use language to talk to another person in an everyday situation.

You will take part in a role play with the examiner. They will first give you a card which has information about the situation for your role play and the roles that you will both play. You have 15 seconds to read the card. The examiner tells you who should start the role play. You have a conversation to do the tasks on your card, but you might also need to think of your own answer to extra questions from the examiner. When you've done all the tasks on your card, the examiner takes the card away from you.

Go to the **Speaking Bank** on page 160–165 *for useful language and practice.*

Go to **Vocabulary maps** on **Pearson English Portal** *for useful language.*

Do **Vocabulary activities** on **Pearson Practice** app *for more practice.*

Watch **Speaking videos** *and do worksheets on* **Pearson English Portal** *to find out more.*

HOW TO DO SECTION 10

What does Section 10 test?

Section 10 tests your speaking ability. It tests how well you can answer questions about yourself and your everyday life and give your opinion (e.g. talking about what you like and don't like).

In this section, you are being tested on:

Your general speaking skills

- If you can describe your everyday life (e.g. people, places, your job or your studies, what you like and don't like).
- If you can join your ideas together in a simple way.

Describing your experiences

- If you can describe events and activities.
- If you can describe plans, routines or activities.
- If you can talk about what you like and don't like about something.
- If you can describe your family, where you live, what you've studied, the job you do now or your last job.
- If you can describe people, places and objects in a simple way.

How to do Section 10

- In this section, you talk about yourself. Remember that you know a lot about your life and what you like and don't like and this should help you to relax.
- Listen to the questions the examiner asks. Take a few seconds to think about your answer before you say anything. If you don't understand a question, ask the examiner to repeat it, by saying something like *Could you say that again, please?*
- One minute is not a lot of time, so make sure you show the examiner how much English you know in your minute. Give as much detail as you can to show the vocabulary you know. If you can, talk about things that happened in the past and things that will happen in the future. This shows the examiner what grammar you know.
- Remember that the first question is short and you only need to give a short answer. The examiner is planning to ask you two or more questions during this section of the exam. You should try to make your answers to these questions longer.
- If the examiner asks you what you like or don't like or what you think about something, use words like *because* or *so* to explain why you like or don't like it.

Scoring

You will get marks for how well you can communicate, how you answer questions, for the grammar and vocabulary you use and your pronunciation. The three speaking sections are 25% of the total score for the whole test.

Timing

You have 1.5 minutes for this section of the test and you have to speak for 1 minute.

SECTION 10: TRAINING

Focus on the instructions

1   Read the Section 10 instructions and questions on page 49.

  a How long does this section last?

  b Do you speak on your own or is it a conversation with the examiner?

  c What sorts of things will you talk about? Can you give some examples?

  d How long do you speak for? Why is this shorter than the whole section?

Focus on the questions

1   Read all Section 10 questions on page 49. Which questions ask you about what you like or don't like?

2   Look at question 1 in the first topic. What do you need to say in your answer?

  a Why you like a food.

  b The food you like the most.

  c Something you don't like to eat.

3   Look at question 2 in the first topic. Which food do you need to talk about?

  a Only your favourite food.

  b The food you never eat.

  c Different kinds of food that you eat.

4   Look at the extra questions for Topic 1.

  a Which question is about what you like to do?

  b Which question is about the past?

  c Which question is about what you normally do or when you do things?

5   Look at question 1 in the second topic. What is a phrase you could use in your answer?

  a by car

  b with my family

  c almost every year

6   The examiner asks: *What is your favourite day of the week?* What's the best answer?

  a I don't have a favourite day of the week.

  b I really like Friday.

  c Saturday is my favourite day because I have time to do sport.

7   Look at the two questions in the third topic. What differences are there between the first and second questions. Choose two answers.

  a You can answer the first question with only a few words.

  b You can answer the second question with only a few words.

  c The first question asks for more details than the second question.

  d The second question asks for more details than the first question.

8   Look at the extra questions for Topic 3.

  a Which question(s) is about what you do at different times?

  b Which question(s) is about the past?

  c Which question(s) is about what you like and don't like?

Focus on the language

1   Which phrase could you use in your answer to the question: *How often do you travel to different places?*

  a by train

  b because it's fun

  c almost every year

2   Find the questions on page 49 that are about the past. Underline the word(s) which tell you the question is about the past.

3   The examiner could ask you *Why?* or *Why not?* at the end of a question. What does the examiner want you to do?

  a Give more detailed information.

  b Give a reason for your answer.

  c Give an example of something you dislike.

4   Which word could you use when you're answering the question *Why?*

  a because

  b but

  c than

Section 10 (1.5 minutes)

Personal information

Examiner:
Now, I'd like you to speak on your own for about 1 minute.

In the test, the examiner might ask you about any different topics. Here are four examples of topics they could ask you about.

TOPIC 1: Food

Question 1
- **What's your favourite food?**

Question 2
- **Tell me about the food you eat.**

> **Extra questions**
> - Do you like cooking? Why/Why not?
> - How often do you eat in restaurants or cafés?
> - What did you eat yesterday?
> - Who do you usually eat your meals with?

TOPIC 2: Travel

Question 1
- **How often do you travel to different places?**

Question 2
- **What's your favourite way to travel?**

> **Extra questions**
> - How did you get here today?
> - How do you usually travel around?
> - Do you enjoy travelling to new places? Why/Why not?
> - What do you do on long journeys?

TOPIC 3: Habits and Routines

Question 1
- **Do you always get up and go to bed at the same time?**

Question 2
- **What are some of the things you do every day?**

> **Extra questions**
> - What is your favourite day of the week?
> - What did you do yesterday?
> - Do you like getting up early? Why/Why not?
> - How are your weekends different from your weekdays?

TOPIC 4: Museums

Question 1
- **Do you enjoy going to museums? Why/Why not?**

Question 2
- **Tell me about a museum that you know.**

> **Extra questions**
> - How often do you visit museums?
> - When do you usually go to a museum?
> - Who do you usually go to a museum with?
> - Do you think museums should be free to enter?

HOW TO DO SECTION 12

What does Section 12 test?

Section 12 tests your speaking ability. It tests how well you can describe what is happening in a picture and answer questions about the picture.

In this section, you are being tested on:

Your general speaking skills

- If you can describe your everyday life, e.g. people, places, your job or your studies, what you like and don't like.
- If you can join your ideas together in a simple way

How to do Section 12

- You will have a few seconds to look at the picture before you have to start talking about it. Look at the picture carefully and think about who the people in the picture are, where they are and what they are doing.
- Decide which part of the picture you're going to talk about first (e.g. The people in the picture). Say everything you can about that part of the picture, and then say everything you can about another part of the picture. Continue like this until you have talked about everything you can see.
- If you aren't sure what to say about the picture, think about the *who*, the *what*, the *how* and the *where* of what you see. If you stop talking, the examiner will ask you questions that start with these words, like *Where are the people? What is the weather like?* So have these questions in your head and answer them when you're talking on your own.
- The examiner will expect you to use the present continuous tense to describe what is happening in the picture, so make sure you know how to use this tense correctly.
- Try to use linking words to connect the things you say to each other, so it doesn't sound like you're just reading a list. For example, you can use *because* or *so* to say what you think the people in the picture are doing, or words like *then* to go from one idea to the next.
- Remember that if the examiner asks you a question, that doesn't mean that you've done something wrong or there's a problem. The examiner is just trying to get you to speak for as long as possible (up until the end of the 1 minute you have to speak) so that they can use what they hear to give you a fair score.

Scoring

You will get marks for how well you can communicate, how you answer questions, for the grammar and vocabulary you use and your pronunciation. The three speaking sections are 25% of the total score for the whole test.

Timing

You have 2 minutes for this section of the test and you have to speak for 1 minute.

SECTION 12: TRAINING

Focus on the instructions

1 Read the Section 12 instructions on page 52.

  a What will the examiner give you at the start of this section?

  b What do you tell the examiner?

  c How long do you have to speak on your own?

  d What kind of questions could the examiner ask you if you stop speaking?

Focus on the questions

1 Read the instructions for 12A and 12B. When the examiner says *Please tell me what you can see*, you need to describe

  a the things, people, or place in the picture.

  b what the people in the picture are doing.

2 When the examiner asks you *what is happening*, you need to describe

  a the things, people, or place in the picture.

  b what the people in the picture are doing.

3 Which question about the picture asks you to describe someone's clothes?

  a What is he/she wearing?

  b What is he/she doing?

4 Which question about the picture asks you to describe something that will happen in the future?

  a What is he/she going to buy?

  b What is he/she doing?

Focus on the language

1 Look at the picture for task 12A on page 155. Write the first ten words you think of that describe what you can see in the picture.

2 Now look at the picture for 12B on page 155. Write the first ten words you think of that describe what is happening in the picture.

3 If the examiner asks you what someone in the picture is going to do, you need to use

  a the present simple tense.

  b the present continuous tense.

  c a future tense.

4 Look at these two sentences you could say when describing a picture:

  1) *There's a man who's wearing a suit and tie, and carrying a briefcase.*

  2) *He's going to buy a newspaper.*

  a Which sentence is about what will happen in the future?

  b Which sentence is about what's happening now?

5 Look at this sentence for describing a picture:

  They are all listening to the guide, who is standing at the front.

  Underline the word that shows you are giving extra information about the guide.

6 Look at these two sentences for describing a picture. Underline all the words for clothes:

  She looks quite young, and she's wearing jeans and a shirt with flowers on it, and a hat. There's a man who's wearing a suit and tie, and carrying a briefcase.

Section 12A (2 minutes)

Picture

Examiner:

Now, here is a picture of some people in a city. Please tell me what you can see and what is happening in the picture.

(Turn to page 155 for your picture.)

Alright? Begin now please.

 about 1 minute

The examiner might ask you more questions to help you talk about the picture.

> **Extra questions:**
> - How many people can you see?
> - Where are they?
> - What is he/she wearing?
> - What is he/she doing?
> - What is he going to buy?
>
> *about 1 minute*

Section 12B (2 minutes)

Picture

Examiner:
Now, here is a picture of people in a street. Please tell me what you can see and what is happening in the picture.

(Turn to page 155 for your picture.)

Alright? Begin now please.

 about 1 minute

The examiner might ask you more questions to help you talk about the picture.

> **Extra questions:**
> - Where are the people?
> - How many people can you see?
> - What are the boys going to do?
> - What has she got?
> - Which bus are the women waiting for?
>
> *about 1 minute*

HOW TO DO SECTION 13

What does Section 13 test?

Section 13 of the paper tests your speaking skills and how well you take part in a conversation. You have a task to complete and you have to answer the examiner's questions.

> **In this section, you are being tested on:**
> **General conversation skills**
> - If you can take part in short conversations in different situations and use common phrases.
> - If you can understand topics you know well.
> - If you can ask for and give information in a simple way.
> - If you can make requests and give your opinion in a simple way.
> - If you can say how you feel in a simple way and say *thank you*.
> - If you can make invitations and reply to them.
> - If you can say if you have or don't have the same opinion as someone else.
> - If you can discuss how to do everyday activities.
> - If you can discuss what to do, where to go and make plans to meet someone.
> - If you can be polite.

How to do Section 13

> - Try to stay relaxed while you're doing the role play. Practise doing role plays before the test.
> - Remember that the examiner isn't interested in how well you can act when you're doing a role play. The examiner just wants to know how well you can communicate with another person.
> - Remember that you have 15 seconds to read the test-taker's card and prepare for this task. Use this time to read the information on the card carefully and think about what to say.
> - Focus on the verbs at the start of each line on the card while you're preparing for the role play. Check with yourself that you understand them before you start speaking and don't be afraid to ask the examiner to repeat something if you don't understand it the first time.
> - The verbs on the test-taker's card will tell you to do some different things that you should know how to do at this level. Start by greeting the examiner, by saying *Hello* or *Good morning*.
> - You will have to show the examiner you know how to ask for information (e.g. *Ask what time the afternoon class starts* or *Find out how long the class is*) or give information (e.g. *Say when the party is*).
> - At the end of the role play, you may have to say thank you to the examiner for something the examiner has done for you (e.g. *Thank your friend*).
> - Focus on doing the things on your card, but remember to listen to the examiner too. You might need to think of your own answer to a question from the examiner. You might also need to say something that isn't on your card because somebody would say it in a real conversation.

Scoring

> You will get marks for how well you can communicate, how you answer questions, for the grammar and vocabulary you use and your pronunciation. The three speaking sections are 25% of the total score for the whole test.

Timing

> You have 1.5 minutes for this section of the test and you have to speak for 1 minute.

SECTION 13: TRAINING

Focus on the instructions

1   Read the Section 13 instructions on page 55.

   a What will the examiner give you at the start of this section?

   b How much time do you have to read it?

   c Who speaks first in this role play: you or the examiner?

   d How many of the things on your card will you do during the role play?

   e How long will you and the examiner talk for?

Focus on the questions

1   Read the questions for 13A and 13B on page 55.

   a When do you greet the examiner?

   b When do you say goodbye to the examiner?

   c When do you need to thank the examiner?

   d If you have to give the examiner some information, where will you find this information?

   e What other questions could the examiner ask you?

2   Choose the correct endings to this sentence. (Choose 3 answers.)

You might need to ask the examiner

   a for advice.

   b to do something for you.

   c to help you with the task.

   d for some information.

Focus on the language

1   Which phrase could you use to greet the examiner at the start of the role play?

   a Excuse me

   b Good morning

   c My name's ...

2   **a** Underline the words you can always use to ask about the price of something.

     How much does that ticket cost?

   b What is another way to ask a question about the price of a ticket?

3   Which phrase can you use to say you want to buy something?

   a Do you know ...?

   b Give me a ...

   c I'd like a ...

4   You say to the examiner: *You can bring sandwiches*. Underline the word which means this is possible.

5   You say to the examiner: *Here is a book he might enjoy*. Underline the word which means this is possible, but you aren't sure.

6   Which phrase can you say when you give someone something?

   a I'll have it.

   b Here you are.

   c Thanks very much.

Section 13A (1.5 minutes)

 Role play

Examiner:

**Now, we are going to take part in a role play. Here is a card with the situation on it.
Please read it to yourself.**

🕐 *15 seconds*

Now let's begin.

Test taker's card

You want to buy a ticket to go on a trip on a tour boat. The examiner is the
ticket seller in the tour boat office.

- Greet the ticket seller.
- Say you want to buy a ticket for the tour boat.
- Find out the time of the afternoon boat.
- Ask about the ticket price.
- Agree to buy the ticket.

(*Turn to page 150 for examiner's card.*)

Section 13B (1.5 minutes)

 Role play

Examiner:

**Now, we are going to take part in a role play. Here is a card with the situation on it.
Please read it to yourself.**

🕐 *15 seconds*

Now let's begin.

Test taker's card

You want to buy a present in a bookshop. The examiner is the bookshop
manager.

- Greet the manager.
- Say who you want to buy a book for.
- Explain what they like reading about.
- Ask the price of the book.
- Say you'd like to buy it.

(*Turn to page 150 for examiner's card.*)

TEST 2 (with guidance)

Section 1

Questions 1–10

▶ You have 10 seconds to read each question. Listen and put a cross ☒ in the box next to the correct answer, as in the example. You have 10 seconds to choose the correct option.

Example What activity is she describing?

A ☒   B ☐   C ☐

1   What kind of fruit will the man buy?

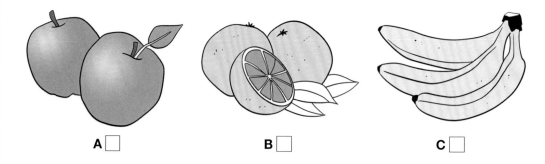

A ☐   B ☐   C ☐

2   Where is the park?

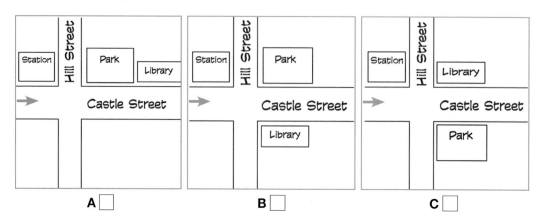

A ☐   B ☐   C ☐

3 What do they need to take on the activity holiday?

A ☐

B ☐

C ☐

4 What will they do in their next English lesson?

A ☐

B ☐

C ☐

5 Where will the boy be on Saturday afternoon?

A ☐

B ☐

C ☐

6 Who is the girl's neighbour?

A ☐

B ☐

C ☐

TIP STRIP

Listening for key words is very important. They can give you clues to finding the correct answers.

Question 3: What sport will they do? Do they need to take things to wear for that? Why don't they need to take riding hats?

Question 4: Listen for *in our next lesson ....* What can you do to prepare for it? What will you do in class?

Question 5: Listen carefully for opposites to the answer. What can't the boy do? Why?

Question 6: Who lives *near* the girl?

Section 1

7 Which concert is the man booking tickets for?

A ☐   B ☐   C ☐

8 What time will flight FY934 leave?

A ☐   B ☐   C ☐

9 What free gift can customers get?

A ☐   B ☐   C ☐

10 What is the man asking staff to do?

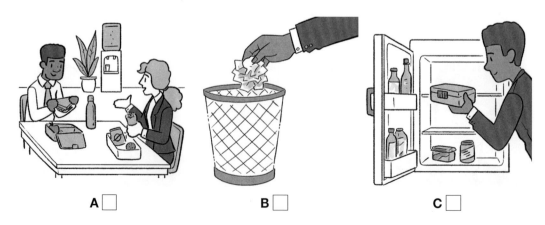

A ☐   B ☐   C ☐

TIP STRIP

In this section, it is important to listen for key words, phrases or details that you see in the question, as they can help you find the correct answer.

Question 7: What concert doesn't the man want tickets for?

Question 8: Listen for a word which means the same as *leave*.

Question 9: Listen for something that is free when you spend more than £20.

Question 10: Listen for the problem. What is it? Does this tell you what the staff need to do?

Section 2

Question 11

▶ You will hear a recording about the weather. Listen to the whole recording once.
Then you will hear the recording again with pauses for you to write down what you hear.
Make sure you spell the words correctly.

TIP STRIP

This dictation gives
some news about today's
weather. What was
closed? Why? What will
happen tomorrow?

After you have listened,
read the sentences and
make sure the grammar
is correct and check
your spelling carefully.

Section 3

Questions 12–16

▶ You will hear a woman called Jessica Murray talking about a college trip. First, read the notes below. Then listen and complete the notes with information from her talk. You will hear the recording twice.

Example Date of trip to London: .... *25th* .... June

12 Time bus leaves: .... a.m.

13 First activity in London: visit a ....

14 Place for lunch: a ....

15 Tour of London: travel by ....

16 Jessica's phone number: 0788 ....

TIP STRIP

Listen carefully as some of the information you will hear might be similar to words you are listening for.

Question 12: Listen for the time the bus leaves, not the time to arrive at the college.

Question 13: What will they do as soon as they arrive in London? Listen for the word that tells you this.

Question 14: Listen for where they will have lunch.

Question 15: Listen for how they are going to do a city tour of London. It could be different to what you might think it is!

Question 16: Write the numbers (1, 2, 3, etc., not the words one, two, three, etc.) as you hear them. There are some double numbers.

Section 3

Questions 17–21

▶ You will hear a telephone conversation. First, read the text below. Then listen and complete the text with information from the conversation. You will hear the recording twice.

Example Message for the school ....*manager*.........., Jane Smith.

Richard **17** .... phoned. He can't come to work today because his

18 .... is ill. He works in the school **19** .... He also won't

be able to go to the **20** .... tonight. He will come back to work on

21 ....

TIP STRIP

Remember to look at the words next to the gaps. They can help you!

Question 17: Listen for his surname. You hear the spelling.

Question 18: Look at the two words after gap 18. Do they help you to know if you are looking for a place, a person or a thing?

Question 19: Look at the beginning of the sentence *He works in the school...* What kind of word fits next? A noun? A verb? An adjective?

Question 20: What information are you listening for here? Could it be something happening at the school?

Question 21: Listen for a day of the week. But be careful – you will hear two days. How do you know which is the right one?

Section 4

Questions 22–26

Read each text and put a cross ☒ by the missing word or phrase, as in the example.

Example

> # Orange Bank
>
> **Open an account today and watch your money ....!**
>
> **Talk to our manager or check our website for more information.**

A ☒ grow

B ☐ save

C ☐ sell

TIP STRIP

Read the information in each text carefully. The words in the text give you clues.

Question 22: The sign in the train station says *we are sorry*. Why might a train station need to say sorry to people?

Question 23: The sign is about doing an activity with other people. Which word or phrase means *come together with other people*?

22

> Because of the heavy snow, the train from Manchester will .... We are sorry about this. It will arrive on platform four at 16:45.

A ☐ be late

B ☐ arrive on time

C ☐ leave soon

23

> Do you love painting and drawing? Do you want to make new friends? .... us at Trenton Art Club on Wednesday evenings.
> 8 p.m., Trenton College.

A ☐ Take part

B ☐ Join

C ☐ Introduce

24

> ## Shop closed
>
> While we .... a problem with our machines, please visit our Madden Road supermarket instead. We will be open again tomorrow.

A ☐ fix

B ☐ make

C ☐ look for

25

> Wait three hours before painting again. The walls must be dry.
>
> Walls which are still a little .... are difficult to paint.

A ☐ warm

B ☐ light

C ☐ wet

26

Welcome to Plumford United Football Club. Enjoy drinks in the club café but please do not .... them to your seats during the game.

A ☐ have

B ☐ take

C ☐ buy

Section 5

Questions 27–31

For each question, put a cross ☒ in the box below the correct picture, as in the example.

Example

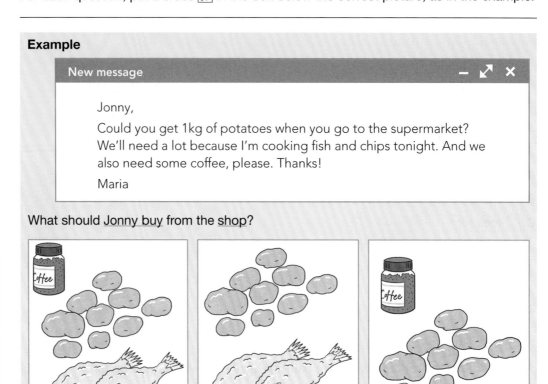

New message

Jonny,
Could you get 1kg of potatoes when you go to the supermarket? We'll need a lot because I'm cooking fish and chips tonight. And we also need some coffee, please. Thanks!
Maria

What should <u>Jonny buy</u> from the <u>shop</u>?

A ☐   B ☐   C ☒

27   What can people buy in the shop's summer sale?

Brooks Store Summer Sale: July–August

10% off all books – great for the beach!

15% off all jeans and shoes

Coming in September: don't miss our beautiful new autumn coats and hats!

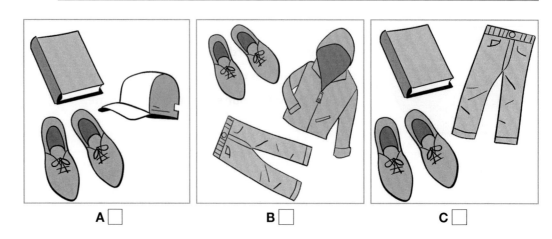

A ☐   B ☐   C ☐

28 What is Julia going to do immediately when she arrives at her new flat?

New message   − ⤢ ✕

Tom,

Thanks for the picture, it'll look great in my new bedroom. I've already packed all my boxes – I can't wait to get to my new flat next week! The first thing I'll do is clean it so that it's ready for a party!

Julia

A ☐

B ☐

C ☐

TIP STRIP

A lot of the words in the text can also be the same as things in the pictures. Make sure you focus on the most important ones.

Question 28: The question is asking about the future. What has Julia already finished doing? Will she do other things before she cleans the flat next week?

Question 29: You need to find something that the restaurant has changed, so you are looking for something on the menu which the restaurant hasn't sold before. Which word describes something different?

29 What has the restaurant changed on the menu?

Lockley's Restaurant

Chicken and rice: cooked the same great way for over fifty years! £16

Fish and vegetables: our most famous dish! £20

Don't miss our lovely new chocolate cake – you'll love it! £6

Coffee Club: Wednesday 12.00-16.00 – Buy one hot drink, get a second free!

A ☐

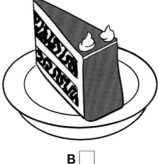

B ☐

C ☐

Section 5

30 Which club can all students join this term?

> ### Student clubs
>
> The last day to join a school club this term is September 5th. The music club is already full but there are other clubs you can join:
>
> Art club: Painting and drawing.
> Wednesdays 15.00–16.00
> Football club: We need girls to join the Year 9 team.
> Tuesdays 17.00–19.00

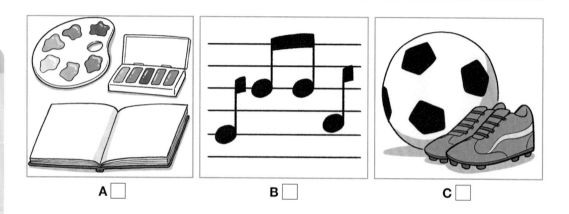

A ☐   B ☐   C ☐

31 How do most students at Erdley School travel to school?

> ### Travel project
>
> For my project, I asked students in my town how they travel. Seventy-two percent of Kings' School students go by car. Erdley School has a free school bus which most pupils use. Twelve percent of students go by bike but the number is growing.

A ☐   B ☐   C ☐

Section 6

Questions 32–35

Read the newspaper article below and answer the questions.

Schoolgirl **Darcy Dawson** is becoming a skiing star! It's her first international competition next month, just after her fourteenth birthday. The other skiers will be sixteen or older so it's a difficult competition. Darcy might not win, but she's excited about taking part to learn new skills.

Darcy's home town is in the south where there aren't any mountains, so she practises in the north. A local gym is paying for her travel costs so she can also practise abroad.

Example What sport does Darcy Dawson do?

............................*skiing*............................

32   How old will Darcy be when she takes part in an international competition?

    ....

33   Why does Darcy want to do the competition?

    ....

34   In which part of the country does Darcy live?

    ....

35   Who is helping Darcy?

    ....

TIP STRIP

Remember to underline the *wh* and *h* words in the questions to help you find the right information.

Question 32: Which sentence gives information about Darcy's age?

Question 33: To find the answer, you need to look for a sentence that describes why she wants to do the competition. What does *excited* mean?

Question 34: Which word in the article means *a place where you come from*? What does the article say about this place? Where is it?

Question 35: Look at the last sentence in the article. What type of help is Darcy getting? Where is she getting this help from? How do you know?

Section 6

Questions 36–39

Read the email below and answer the questions.

New message

Hi Steve,

I'm enjoying my new job in Madrid. I'm even taking Spanish classes! I share a flat with two university students. It's perfect because it's in the city centre. I go to work by bus, but I take the train to get to my lessons.

The lessons are great because I can use the new words in my daily life. But the best thing is meeting other people. We speak different languages so we always use Spanish together!

Joe

Example What course is Joe doing?

.... *Spanish* ....

36 Who does Joe live with?

....

37 Why does Joe like his accommodation?

....

38 How does Joe travel to his course?

....

39 What does Joe enjoy most about his course?

....

TIP STRIP

Sometimes words from the text aren't in the questions. You need to look for similar words.

Question 36: Which verb do we use when we live in accommodation with other people?

Question 37: Look at the sentence *it's perfect*. What is *it* talking about?

Question 38: What other words in the text could mean *course*? Can you see a way of travelling near one of these words? Read this part carefully.

Question 39: Which words in the text show what Joe thinks of his course? Which phrase in the text means *like the most*? Read this sentence carefully to find the answer.

Questions 40–46

Read the letter from the class teacher and complete the notes. Write **no more than three words** from the letter in each gap.

Trip to the Computer Museum

Our class trip to the Computer Museum is next Tuesday, 14th November. We're going there by coach, so it's very important you aren't late. You must be at school by 8.45 a.m as we leave at 9.15 a.m. The journey to the museum takes 50 minutes.

At the museum, you'll see some very big computers used in the 1960s and find out how they have changed over time. For this month only, you'll be able to see an exhibition of the first mobile phones.

You'll discover the games your parents played when they were your age and why computer games have become so popular. And while you're there, you'll even learn how to make one!

Finally, you need to bring your own lunch because the museum doesn't have a café. If the weather is good, we can eat in the outdoor picnic area.

Example The class trip is to the: .... *Computer Museum* ....

40 Date of the trip: ....

41 We will travel by: ....

42 We will leave school at: ....

43 We will see some very old computers from: ....

44 There will be a special exhibition about: ....

45 You will learn how to make a: ....

46 You must remember to take: ....

TIP STRIP

Remember you will find the answers in the text in the same order as the questions.

Question 40: Look for details about the trip.

Question 41: Where can you find a word that describes how to travel?

Question 42: The preposition *at* is often followed by a time.

Question 43: Find the paragraph that talks about computers.

Question 44: Find an expression that tells you about an exhibition.

Question 45: Look for a sentence about making something.

Question 46: Is there another way of saying *You need to bring*?

Section 8

Question 47

Use the information in **Section 7** to help you write your answer.

You have read your teacher's letter about the trip to the Computer Museum. Now write an email to your friend. Write **50–70 words** and include the following information:

- Say where you're going and what you're going to do there.
- Tell your friend what you like about class trips.
- Ask your friend how he/she feels about class trips.

TIP STRIP

- Underline the important words in the question about the information you need to include, like, *Computer Museum, what you like about class trips* and *how he/she feels*. These will give you the *where, why* and *how* and *what* you need to write about.
- Write down some ideas for each bullet point in the question.
- Pay attention to the kind of text you need to write. What kinds of words or phrases will you need to use?
- Write the email. Make sure you include information about all three prompts in your email. Don't forget to begin with *Hi/Dear* + your friend's name and end the email with your name.
- Check that you've written between 50 and 70 words.
- Check your grammar and spelling.

Question 48

Choose **one** of the topics below and write your answer in **80–100 words**.

Either:

A Films

You and your friend decided to go and see a film last Saturday. Look at the pictures and write a story about what happened.

Or:

B Work

Last week, a journalist came to your school to give a talk about her work. Look at the pictures and write a description about her job for your diary.

Put a cross X in the box next to the task you have chosen.

A ☐   B ☐

TIP STRIP

- Read both questions carefully and look at each set of pictures.
- Do you have enough ideas to write about both options? Choose option A if you know some vocabulary about going to the cinema, or option B if you are more interested in writing about travel.

Option A: Imagine that you and a friend saw a film and describe what happened. Include information about what you did in each picture (e.g. *we met for a coffee, we saw an interesting film poster, we bought some tickets*).

Option B: For this question, you can use present tenses as well as past tenses because you are writing about a journalist's job, her trip to China and what happened afterwards. Look at each picture and make notes about some of the things she must do for her job.

TEST 2

WRITING (with guidance)

Personal information

Examiner:
Now, I'd like you to speak on your own for about 1 minute.

In the test, the examiner might ask you about any different topics. Here are four examples of topics they could ask you about.

TOPIC 1: Music

Question 1
- **How often do you listen to music?**

Question 2
- **What sort of music do people your age usually listen to?**

Extra questions
- Where do you usually listen to music?
- Can anyone in your family play an instrument?
- Have you ever been to a concert?
- Do you buy music on the internet?

TOPIC 2: Hobbies

Question 1
- **How much free time do you have?**

Question 2
- **Tell me about your hobbies.**

Extra questions
- What hobby would you like to start doing? Why?
- What hobbies do other people in your family have?
- Why do you enjoy your hobby?
- Do you think your hobby is easy?

TOPIC 3: Place where you live

Question 1
- **Do you live in a town or city, or in the countryside?**

Question 2
- **Can you tell me about where you live?**

Extra questions
- What is your favourite street where you live?
- What kinds of shops are there where you live?
- What is there for young people to do where you live?
- Where do tourists go when they visit the place where you live?

TOPIC 4: Clothes

Question 1
- **What kind of clothes do you like wearing?**

Question 2
- **What colour clothes do you like wearing?**

Extra questions
- Do you wear the same things at the weekend and in the week?
- Where do you buy different clothes for different seasons?
- Do you enjoy shopping for clothes?
- Do you keep your clothes for a long time?

TIP STRIP

- In the test the examiner will ask you one short question, followed by more questions to help you continue to talk.
- The questions in Section 10 will be about general topics about you, your family or other people you know, and the place where you live.
- You only need to give short answers to the first questions the examiner will ask you in this section, but make sure you say more than just yes or *no*.
- Make sure you answer the examiner's questions, and don't start talking about other things.
- Remember to use your own real experiences to talk about things you know.

Section 12A (2 minutes)

Picture

Examiner:

Now, here is a picture of people in a park. Please tell me what you can see and what is happening in the picture.

(*Turn to page 156 for your picture.*)

Alright? Begin now please.

 about 1 minute

Extra questions:

- Where are the people?
- What are the teenagers doing?
- What is the little girl doing?

- How many birds are there?
- What do they sell in the café?

 *about 1 minute*

TIP STRIP 12A

- Start by talking about the places, people or objects you can see. Which of these things can you see in the picture for 12A?
- Talk about how many people you can see and what they are doing in more detail. You should also describe what they are wearing, and about their feelings. Do they look happy, or sad, for example?
- You can talk about the relationships between the people. Could they be friends, or mother and daughter?
- You can talk about any extra information you find in the picture (e.g. times, prices, or even the weather).

Section 12B (2 minutes)

Picture

Examiner:

Now, here is a picture of some people relaxing. Please tell me what you can see and what is happening in the picture.

(*Turn to page 156 for your picture.*)

Alright? Begin now please.

 about 1 minute

Extra questions:

- Where are the people?
- What is the woman reading?
- What is the boy doing?

- What time is it?
- What is the man wearing?

 *about 1 minute*

TIP STRIP 12B

- Start by talking about the place, and the people or objects you can see. For example, a living room, with a man, a woman and a teenage boy. You should describe what they are each doing and what they are wearing.
- There is also furniture that you can describe (e.g. the sofa, and the TV, as well as things like the plate of biscuits, the computer tablet, and the woman's phone on the chair). Don't forget to talk about what you can see on the TV, and the time on the clock on the wall.

Section 13A (1.5 minutes)

Role play

Examiner:

Now, we are going to take part in a role play. Here is a card with the situation on it. Please read it to yourself.

🕐 *about 15 seconds*

> **Test taker's card**
>
> You want to do a tennis class at your local sports centre. The examiner is the sports centre receptionist.
> * Greet the receptionist and ask for information about tennis classes.
> * Ask what time the afternoon class starts.
> * Find out how long the class is.
> * Ask when you need to pay for the class.
> * Thank the receptionist.

(*Turn to page 151 for examiner's card.*)

TIP STRIP 13B

* In this part of the test, you will have a card with some information on it. Use this to have a conversation with the examiner.
* You have 15 seconds to read the information and think about what you want to say or ask.
* You can start with something like: *Hello, I want some information about tennis classes, please.*

Section 13B (1.5 minutes)

Role play

Examiner:

Now, we are going to take part in a role play. Here is a card with the situation on it. Please read it to yourself.

🕐 *about 15 seconds*

> **Test taker's card**
>
> You are at the cinema to buy tickets. The examiner is the ticket seller.
> * Greet the ticket seller.
> * Ask if there are still tickets for the 6 p.m. film.
> * Say how many you want to buy.
> * Find out what snacks you can buy.
> * Say what snacks you want.
> * Thank the ticket seller.

(*Turn to page 151 for examiner's card.*)

TIP STRIP 13B

* The card says *Greet the ticket seller* so all you need to do is say *Hello!* Your first question could be *Are there any tickets for the film at 6 o'clock, please?*
* Give the examiner time to reply before you ask your next question.

TEST 3

Section 1

Questions 1–10

▶ You have 10 seconds to read each question. Listen and put a cross ☒ in the box next to the correct answer, as in the example. You have 10 seconds to choose the correct option.

Example What activity is she describing?

A ☒   B ☐   C ☐

1   Which club will the college have for the first time?

A ☐   B ☐   C ☐

2   Which book does the girl need to get?

A ☐   B ☐   C ☐

3   What is the TV programme about?

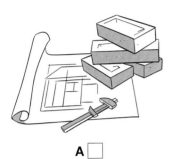

A ☐

B ☐

C ☐

4   What is cheaper than usual this week?

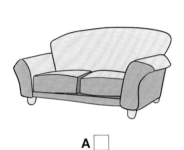

A ☐

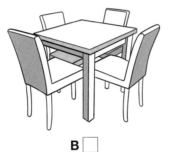

B ☐

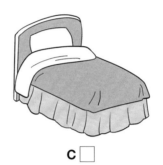

C ☐

5   Where are the speakers?

A ☐

B ☐

C ☐

6   Which apartment are they talking about?

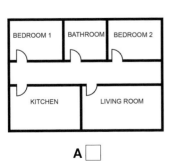

A ☐

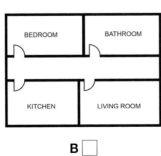

B ☐

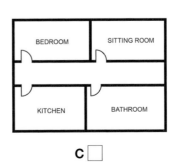

C ☐

Section 1

7   Where did the man stay on holiday?

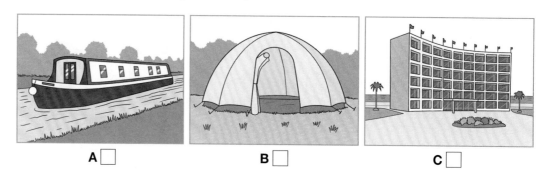

A ☐   B ☐   C ☐

8   What is in the dish that the woman says is really good?

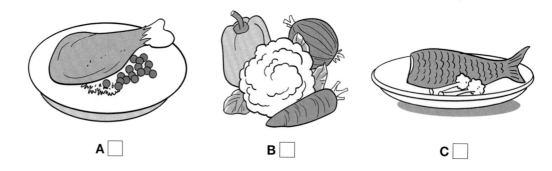

A ☐   B ☐   C ☐

9   What is the girl studying in science classes at the moment?

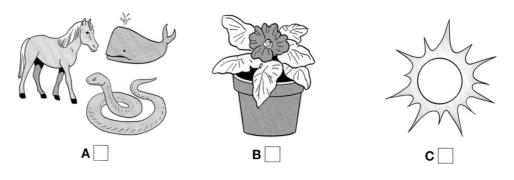

A ☐   B ☐   C ☐

10   How does the man contact his brother?

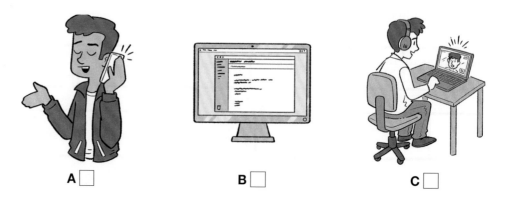

A ☐   B ☐   C ☐

Section 2

Question 11

▶ You will hear a recording about a place. Listen to the whole recording once. Then you will hear the recording again with pauses for you to write down what you hear. Make sure you spell the words correctly.

Section 3

Questions 12–16

▶ You will hear a man giving some information about a day trip. First, read the sentences below. Then listen and complete the sentences with information from his talk. You will hear the recording twice.

Example The Environment Group's beach-cleaning day is on ___17th November___ .

12   The group will clean rubbish from a beach called

.... Sands.

13   The group will travel to the beach by ....

14   Travelling to the beach and back will cost .... for students.

15   There is a lot of .... rubbish on the beach.

16   After cleaning the beach, there will be a ....

Section 3

▶ You will hear a conversation. First, read the notes below. Then listen and complete the notes with information from the conversation. You will hear the recording twice.

Example The women's new flat is: next to the ....*station*.............

17   First day in her new flat: Saturday .... June

18   Address of flat: 10, ... Road

19   Which floor the flat is on: ....

20   Best place to park: in the .... car park

21   What to get for the flat: a ....

Section 4

Questions 22–26

Read each text and put a cross ☒ by the missing word or phrase, as in the example.

Example

New message − ↗ ✕

Dear Maria,
Don't forget to check the homework task on the class website.
You need to .... to me by Friday.
Mr Taylor

A ☒ hand it

B ☐ look it up

C ☐ take it out

22

The **Open Day** is for our students who haven't chosen their .... yet. Try different lessons, and the teachers will help you choose the right course.

A ☐ subjects

B ☐ school

C ☐ classrooms

23

Maybury Shopping Centre

The toilets on the first floor are .... today so please use the toilets on the second floor instead.

A ☐ ready

B ☐ locked

C ☐ open

24

Bobby's Taxis

We need .... to work in the Maldon area on Saturday nights. You must have your own vehicle. Call 0759 689548.

A ☐ engineers

B ☐ drivers

C ☐ pilots

25

How we choose our coffee

We .... the best products for you to enjoy at home by visiting farms all over the world!

A ☐ drink

B ☐ grow

C ☐ find

26

THIS TICKET MACHINE DOESN'T TAKE CASH.

PLEASE USE A CREDIT CARD. CHOOSE YOUR TRAIN TICKET

BY .... ON THE INFORMATION ON THE SCREEN.

A ☐ clicking

B ☐ putting

C ☐ checking

Section 5

Questions 27–31

For each question, put a cross ☒ in the box below the correct picture, as in the example.

Example

> Lucy,
>
> Thanks for looking after my house. My mum's taking the dog out for a walk so don't worry about that. You don't need to do anything in the garden. Could you please just feed the fish in the morning?
>
> Thanks,
>
> Maria

What should Lucy do for Maria?

A ☐   B ☐   C ☒

27   What does Tom need to do today?

> Tom,
>
> The engineer's coming to fix the problem with the internet at 10.00. I'll be back from the supermarket this afternoon, and then you can get the flat ready for the party while I do the cooking.
>
> Andy

A ☐   B ☐   C ☐

Section 5

28 What was Holly's photo project about?

> ### School News
>
> Student Holly White has just won £500 in a national photo project competition. Students around the country took part in the competition and Holly's pictures of birds won. As part of the prize, the school also won some new computers. Congratulations, Holly!

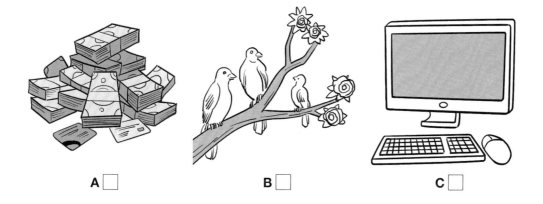

A ☐   B ☐   C ☐

29 What can people see in Great Heston?

> ## Tourist information
>
> Visit the lovely garden at Longton Hall. Then cross over the beautiful old bridge into Great Ripton. Relax in a café by the river. From there, it's only 3km to the village of Great Heston, where you'll find the Moors Art Centre.

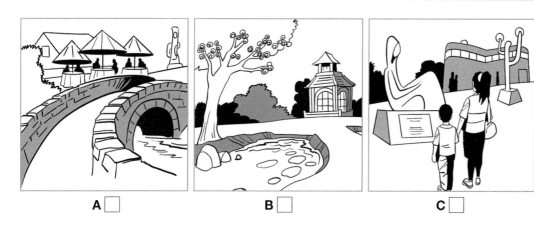

A ☐   B ☐   C ☐

Section 5

30 Which animal may be difficult for visitors to see?

> ### Tourist information
>
> The monkeys play in large groups. They're funny but may steal your lunch!
>
> You might not see the female elephants who are getting ready for the birth of their babies.
>
> The adult lions are protecting their babies. Making noise near them will make them angry.

A ☐

B ☐

C ☐

31 Where does Jenny want to go with Mike?

> Mike,
> Thanks for inviting me out. I don't want to go dancing, but I've heard there's 30 percent off at the Royal Theatre tonight. Let's try that!
> I'm going to the gym soon, but I can meet you in town at 18.30.
> Jenny

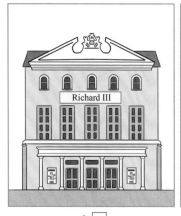
A ☐

B ☐

C ☐

Questions 32–35

Read the blog post below and answer the questions.

I've just been to the local college for *'Start-Up Day'*. It was for students who want to start a business. There were interesting talks but the best part was meeting Leon Jackson. When he was sixteen, he started an online business selling his own pictures. I'd love to do the same but with clothes. He gave me some ideas and even showed me how to build a website. I've decided to start making my business cards. I might need them!

Example Where was the *Start-Up Day* event?

............................the local college............................

32   What did the writer enjoy most about the event?

    ....

33   What product does the writer want to sell?

    ....

34   What did the writer learn to do at the *Start-Up Day* event?

    ....

35   What is the writer planning to do?

    ....

Questions 36–39

Read the newspaper article below and answer the questions.

TVstar Rhea Mills has opened a restaurant by the beach in Padley. Over her twenty-year cooking career, she has worked in many famous restaurants, but this is her first business. Although everyone knows Rhea's TV shows about French cooking, *Rhea's House* is an Indian restaurant. Her father is from Mumbai and taught her to cook. 'My love of food comes from him,' she says. *Rhea's House* is a place with excellent food and service, although not everyone loves the loud music!

Example Where in Padley is Rhea's business?

.................................by the beach..................................

36 How long has Rhea worked in the food industry?

....

37 What food is Rhea famous for?

....

38 Who helped Rhea become interested in cooking?

....

39 What might be a problem for some visitors to the restaurant?

....

Questions 40–46

Read the notice and complete the notes. Write **no more than three words** from the notice in each gap.

School book club

Do you love reading? Then you should join the school's book club called Read Up. This popular club gets together on Fridays and is the perfect way to start your weekend. The 45-minute meetings are in the library. They start at noon and are a great way to hear about new books.

What kinds of books do we discuss at Read Up? All kinds! Last month members read *Blue Sky* and they're reading *The Journey* now. After they've finished that, they'll start reading an exciting story called *Island Boy*. Don't worry, members have three weeks to read each new book before sharing their opinions.

Did you know Read Up is the least expensive club in the whole school? That's because it's free to join! And what's more, the library staff make snacks for members to have at each meeting. What are you waiting for? Join today!

Example Name of book club: .... *Read Up* ....

40 The club meets on: ....

41 Meetings take place in: ....

42 Meetings start at: ....

43 The next book members will read is called: ....

44 Members discuss a new book every: ....

45 Cost to join: ....

46 At every meeting, members have some: ....

Section 8

Question 47

Use the information in **Section 7** to help you write your answer.

You have read the notice about the book club. Now write an email to your friend. Write **50–70 words** and include the following information:

- Tell your friend about the book club and what you can do there.
- Explain why you want to join the club.
- Ask your friend to go to a meeting with you.

Question 48

Choose **one** of the topics below and write your answer in **80–100 words**.

Either:

A Cooking

Last week, your friend made a cake to share with his friends. Write a diary entry about what happened.

Or:

B Restaurants

Last Friday, you went to a new restaurant with some friends from your college. Look at the pictures and write a blog post about it.

Put a cross ☒ in the box next to the task you have chosen.

A ☐   B ☐

TEST 3

WRITING

Section 10 (1.5 minutes)

Personal information

Examiner:
Now, I'd like you to speak on your own for about 1 minute.

In the test, the examiner might ask you about any different topics. Here are four examples of topics they could ask you about.

TOPIC 1: Routines

Question 1
- **Do you prefer weekends or weekdays?**

Question 2
- **Tell me what you usually do at weekends.**

> **Extra questions**
> - Do you like to do different things each weekend?
> - What did you do last weekend?
> - Are you usually busy in the week? Why/Why not?
> - Do you do any work at the weekend?

TOPIC 2: Weather

Question 1
- **What's the weather like today?**

Question 2
- **What's the weather usually like where you live?**

> **Extra questions**
> - What's your favourite type of weather?
> - Do you prefer very hot or very cold weather?
> - Is there any weather you don't like?
> - What do you wear in different sorts of weather?

TOPIC 3: Accommodation

Question 1
- **Do you live in a house or an apartment?**

Question 2
- **What's your house or apartment like?**

> **Extra questions**
> - Who lives with you in your house or apartment?
> - What's your favourite place in your home?
> - Do you think your house is the right size for you?
> - What would you like to buy for your house or your room?

TOPIC 4: Films

Question 1
- **Do you have a favourite film?**

Question 2
- **What kind of films do you like watching?**

> **Extra questions**
> - Do you watch films alone or with others?
> - Do you prefer watching films at the cinema or on TV?
> - Who is your favourite actor?
> - Do you like watching films from other countries?

Section 12A (2 minutes)

Picture

Examiner:

Now, here is a picture of some people in a café. Please tell me what you can see and what is happening in the picture.

(Turn to page 157 for your picture.)

Alright? Begin now please.

 about 1 minute

The examiner might ask you more questions to help you talk about the picture.

> **Extra questions:**
> - How many tables are there?
> - What is the woman wearing?
> - What is the woman doing?
> - What are they eating?
> - What time is it?
>
>  *about 1 minute*

Section 12B (2 minutes)

Picture

Examiner:

Now, here is a picture of people in a town. Please tell me what you can see and what is happening in the picture.

(Turn to page 157 for your picture.)

Alright? Begin now please.

 about 1 minute

The examiner might ask you more questions to help you talk about the picture.

> **Extra questions:**
> - Where are the people?
> - What number is the bus?
> - What is the man wearing?
> - What are the children doing?
> - What is the weather like?
>
>  *about 1 minute*

Section 13A (1.5 minutes)

Examiner:

Now, we are going to take part in a role play. Here is a card with the situation on it. Please read it to yourself.

about 15 seconds

Now let's begin.

> **Test taker's card**
>
> You are organising a party and want your friend to help you. The examiner is your friend.
>
> - Greet your friend and ask them to help with your party.
> - Explain what food they can bring.
> - Say when the party is.
> - Ask if your friend can come early to help.
> - Say what time your friend can come at and ask if it's OK.

(Turn to page 152 for examiner's card.)

Section 13B (1.5 minutes)

Examiner:

Now, we are going to take part in a role play. Here is a card with the situation on it. Please read it to yourself.

about 15 seconds

Now let's begin.

> **Test taker's card**
>
> You are meeting your friend in a café but you're calling your friend to say you'll be late. The examiner is your friend.
>
> - Say who you are and apologise for being late.
> - Explain what happened.
> - Say when you'll arrive.
> - Say goodbye.

(Turn to page 152 for examiner's card.)

Section 1

Questions 1–10

▶ You have 10 seconds to read each question. Listen and put a cross ☒ in the box next to the correct answer, as in the example. You have 10 seconds to choose the correct option.

Example What activity is she describing?

A ☒   B ☐   C ☐

1   Where are the girl and her mum going to go?

A ☐   B ☐   C ☐

2   What will be next on the radio?

A ☐   B ☐   C ☐

3   What does the woman have to wear at work?

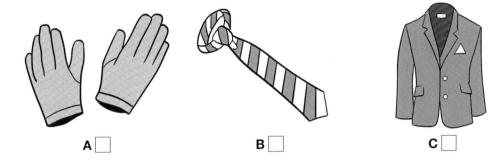

A ☐   B ☐   C ☐

4   What does the man teach people to play?

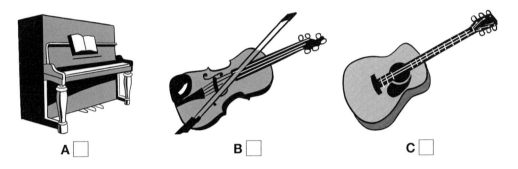

A ☐   B ☐   C ☐

5   Who will teach the science course?

A ☐   B ☐   C ☐

6   What is not working?

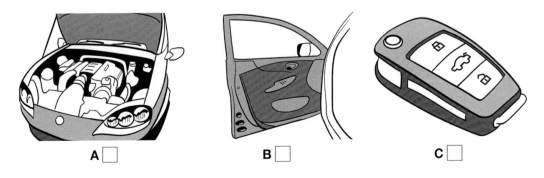

A ☐   B ☐   C ☐

Section 1

7 Which painting did the woman like the most?

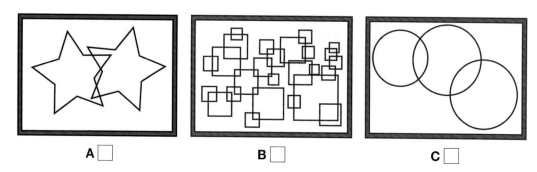

A ☐   B ☐   C ☐

8 What job would the girl like to have?

A ☐   B ☐   C ☐

9 What is on the first floor of the hotel?

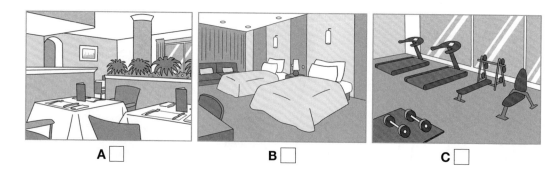

A ☐   B ☐   C ☐

10 What is the Environment Group's new project?

A ☐   B ☐   C ☐

Section 2

Question 11

▶ You will hear a recording about a place. Listen to the whole recording once. Then you will hear the recording again with pauses for you to write down what you hear. Make sure you spell the words correctly.

Section 3

Questions 12–16

▶ You will hear a phone conversation. First, read the notes below. Then listen and complete the notes with information from the conversation. You will hear the recording twice.

Example Number of *Star Gyms* in the city: .... 4 ....

12 Gym in King Street: next to the ....

13 Price per month for students: £..

14 Price doesn't include: ....

15 Usual time gym closes: .... p.m.

16 *King Street Gym* has a: ....

Questions 17–21

▶ You will hear a woman talking about a course. First, read the notes below. Then listen and complete the notes with information from the talk. You will hear the recording twice.

Example Name of painting course teacher: Katie .... *Black* ....

17 Day of evening lessons: ....

18 Art room: in the .... building

19 Date of first lesson: .... January

20 Subject of first lesson: ....

21 Where painting show will be: in the college ....

Section 4

Questions 22–26

Read each text and put a cross ☒ by the missing word or phrase, as in the example.

Example

> **New message**   – ⤢ ✕
>
> Lucy,
>
> I .... your favourite cup – I'm sorry! I tried to fix it but it was just impossible. I'll buy you a new one.
>
> Zoe

A ☒ dropped

B ☐ borrowed

C ☐ lost

22

Visitors must not bring mobile phones into the hall while we make the TV show. Please .... them at reception.

A ☐ give

B ☐ leave

C ☐ receive

23

For Sale

With new lights and lock, this .... is great. The seat moves up and down so it's perfect for children as they grow.

A ☐ bike

B ☐ car

C ☐ boat

24

THE A34 ROAD FROM WILSHAM TO LEMINGSTON
IS CLOSED TODAY. PLEASE CHECK ONLINE TO FIND
A DIFFERENT .... IF YOU ARE DRIVING NORTH.

A ☐ route

B ☐ station

C ☐ vehicle

25

Pet Food

Remember the .... of the cat you are feeding.
To keep them healthy and happy, small cats should
eat less than large cats!

A ☐ shape

B ☐ age

C ☐ size

26

Dear guests,
It is not safe to run near the swimming area.
Accidents can happen .... Also, do not take
glasses into this area.

A ☐ on wet floors

B ☐ under water

C ☐ into the pool

Section 5

Questions 27–31

For each question, put a cross ☒ in the box below the correct picture, as in the example.

Example

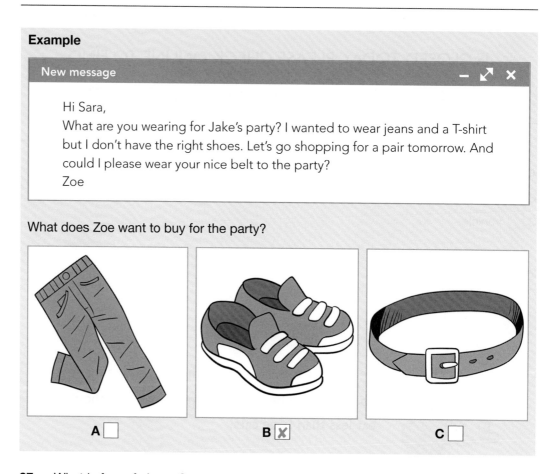

New message   − ↗ ✕

Hi Sara,
What are you wearing for Jake's party? I wanted to wear jeans and a T-shirt but I don't have the right shoes. Let's go shopping for a pair tomorrow. And could I please wear your nice belt to the party?
Zoe

What does Zoe want to buy for the party?

A ☐   B ☒   C ☐

27   What is free of charge?

> Our food tour starts at the market where you can buy local food like our famous Tonbridge cake. After enjoying a free drink at the historic Black Cat café, we'll visit the chocolate factory. Show your tour ticket to get 10 percent off all chocolate at the factory shop.

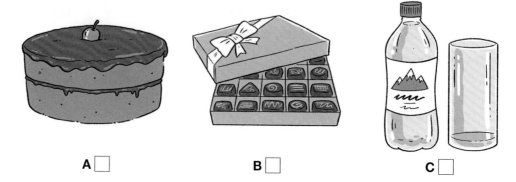

A ☐   B ☐   C ☐

28   Where can Kate find the key to the house?

> **New message**   — ↗ ✕
>
> Kate,
> I've moved the house key. It was under the plant pot by the front door but that wasn't safe! Walk round to the back. The key's behind the bin by the window. If you need the garage key, it's on the kitchen table.
> Nick

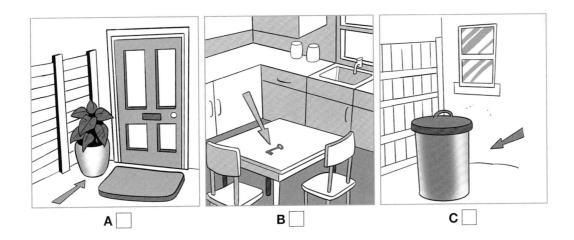

A ☐   B ☐   C ☐

29   What might make it easier for people to sleep in hot weather?

> Spending time in high temperatures can be difficult. Many people find drinking milk helps them sleep when it's very hot. During the day, remember that it's important to drink water. Eating ice-cream will only make you feel better for a short time!

A ☐   B ☐   C ☐

Section 5

30 Which summer activity is for young children and parents to do together?

> ### Summer Activities
>
> **New Moves** (four-week course) – children aged 3–6 learn simple dances. At the end of the course, there's a show for their friends and families.
>
> **Animal Club** – young children love painting animals and parents enjoy helping them!
>
> **Friends Club** – play games and make friends. Children aged 8–12.

A   B   C

31 Which activity is for all students?

> ### Students wanted!
>
> If you're studying to become a teacher, could you help us teach local children computer skills? We also need students to help clean the local park. And, if you can drive, could you help us take books and toys to the children's hospital?

A   B   C

Questions 32–35

Read the college letter below and answer the questions.

Dear Lucy,

We hope you enjoy your science course. Before the term begins, please buy your coursebooks. You'll need them on the first day of class. Once you start your lessons, Jan Williams will be the person to contact for any problems with your classes.

Our college bedrooms are for first-year students and cost £5,000 a year. Students pay £800 before the term starts to book the rooms, and £4,200 later. Second-year students have to rent private accommodation.

Maureen Baxter

Example What is Lucy going to study?

.... *science* ....

32 What should Lucy do before she starts her course?

....

33 Who can students talk to about their courses?

....

34 How much do students have to pay for college accommodation?

....

35 Where do students live after they finish the first year?

....

Section 6

Questions 36–39

Read the newspaper article below and answer the questions.

Would you like to be a football player? Channel Zero's show *Football Dreams* might change your opinion! This programme isn't about famous football stars. It's about players at a small football club. Although the programme is funny, it also shows that it isn't easy to work in the football industry.

People watching the show and women's sports organisations are sad that *Football Dreams* doesn't show female players. However, the TV company is making a programme about female runners. We can't wait to watch it!

Example Who is showing the programme?

Channel Zero

36 What type of football club is the show about?

....

37 What does the programme show in the football industry?

....

38 Why are people unhappy about the show?

....

39 What will the TV company's next show be about?

....

Section 7

Questions 40–46

Read the blog post and complete the notes. Write **no more than three words** from the blog post in each gap.

My first cycling race abroad

My name's Ryan Singer and I belong to a cycling club called Top Speed. I often compete in races in the UK. This summer, my dad let me enter a race in Belgium – my first race abroad.

We went there in my dad's car. First, we went through the Eurotunnel to France, then to Ghent in Belgium where my dad booked a hotel. I went to bed early because I needed to rest before the race. It started at 9.30 a.m. but I woke up at 7 a.m. to get ready.

There were over a hundred cyclists but not everyone was in the same race. I was in the 15–16 age group. There were 53 people in my group and 65 in the 17–18 age group. It wasn't easy, especially because it was very hot that day. I didn't win but everyone got a T-shirt. I wear it all the time!

Example Name of Ryan's cycling club:

.... *Top Speed* ....

40   Country the competition took place in: ....

41   Ryan travelled to the competition by: ....

42   Ryan and his father stayed at: a ....

43   The race began at: ....

44   Number of cyclists in Ryan's race: ....

45   During the race, the weather was: ....

46   Ryan's prize was: a ....

Section 8

Question 47

Use the information in **Section 7** to help you write your answer.

You have read the blog post about a cycling competition. Now write an email to the Top Speed cycling club. Write **50–70 words** and include the following information:

• Say why you want to join the club.
• Tell the club how much cycling experience you have.
• Ask for information about the club.

Question 48

Choose **one** of the topics below and write your answer in **80–100 words**.

Either:

A Picnics

Last weekend, you and your friends had a picnic. Look at the pictures and write a description of what happened in your diary.

Or:

B Art

Lisa is your friend and she loves drawing. She wanted to give her grandfather a special present. Look at the pictures and write a story about what she did.

Put a cross ☒ in the box next to the task you have chosen.

A ☐   B ☐

Section 10 (1.5 minutes)

Personal information

Examiner:
Now, I'd like you to speak on your own for about 1 minute.

In the test, the examiner might ask you about any different topics. Here are four examples of topics they could ask you about.

TOPIC 1: Work

Question 1
- **Is there a job you would really like to do?**

Question 2
- **What do you think is a good job?**

Extra questions
- What jobs do people in your family do?
- Is it good to work near where you live?
- What job would you not want to do?
- Is it good to travel around for your work?

TOPIC 2: Reading

Question 1
- **Do you like reading?**

Question 2
- **What is your favourite book?**

Extra questions
- Do you talk about books with your friends? Why/Why not?
- Did you like reading when you were younger?
- Who is your favourite writer? Why?
- Do you prefer reading books or watching films?

TOPIC 3: Holidays

Question 1
- **Do you like going on holiday?**

Question 2
- **Tell me about your last holiday.**

Extra questions
- How often do you go on holiday?
- Do you go on holiday in your country?
- When is the best time to have a holiday?
- Where do you think is the best place to spend a holiday? Why?

TOPIC 4: Animals

Question 1
- **Do you like animals?**

Question 2
- **What is your favourite animal?**

Extra questions
- Are TV programmes about animals popular where you live?
- What animals can you see on farms in your country?
- Have you got a pet?
- What kind of animal is a good pet?

Section 12A (2 minutes)

Picture

Examiner:

Now, here is a picture of some young people in a room. Please tell me what you can see and what is happening in the picture.

(Turn to page 158 for your picture.)

Alright? Begin now please.

🕐 *about 1 minute*

The examiner might ask you more questions to help you talk about the picture.

Extra questions:
- Where are the people?
- How many people are in the room?
- What are the women doing?
- What can you see on the table?
- What can you see on the bookcase?
- What is the man wearing?

 🕐 *about 1 minute*

Section 12B (2 minutes)

Picture

Examiner:

Now, here is a picture of people outside. Please tell me what you can see and what is happening in the picture.

(Turn to page 158 for your picture.)

Alright? Begin now please.

🕐 *about 1 minute*

The examiner might ask you more questions to help you talk about the picture.

Extra questions:
- Where are the people?
- What are the people wearing?
- How many animals can you see?
- What is in the sky?
- What can you see next to this field?
- What are the people eating?

🕐 *about 1 minute*

Section 13A (1.5 minutes)

Role play

Examiner:

Now, we are going to take part in a role play. Here is a card with the situation on it. Please read it to yourself.

about 15 seconds

Now let's begin.

> **Test taker's card**
>
> Your friend Sam is having a party this weekend and you are going. The examiner is another friend of yours who is also going to the party.
>
> - Greet your friend.
> - Tell your friend what time Sam's party starts.
> - Say what present you are taking, and why you chose it.
> - Explain how you're getting to the party and ask if your friend wants to come with you.
> - Say goodbye.

(*Turn to page 153 for examiner's card.*)

Section 13B (1.5 minutes)

Role play

Examiner:

Now, we are going to take part in a role play. Here is a card with the situation on it. Please read it to yourself.

about 15 seconds

Now let's begin.

> **Test taker's card**
>
> You want to catch a train and need some help. The examiner is a station worker on the platform.
>
> - Greet the station worker and ask when the next train to the city leaves.
> - Find out which platform it goes from.
> - Ask where you get your tickets from.
> - Find out when the station café closes.
> - Thank the station worker and say goodbye.

(*Turn to page 153 for examiner's card.*)

Section 1

Questions 1–10

▶ You have 10 seconds to read each question. Listen and put a cross ☒ in the box next to the correct answer, as in the example. You have 10 seconds to choose the correct option.

Example What activity is she describing?

A ☒   B ☐   C ☐

1   Where should train passengers put their bags?

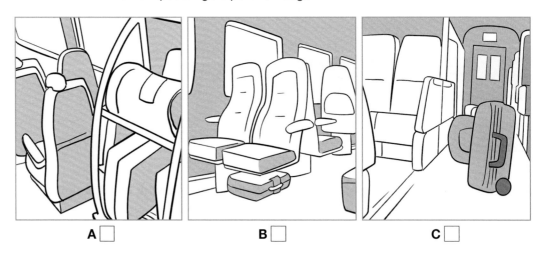

A ☐   B ☐   C ☐

2   What will the weather be like tomorrow?

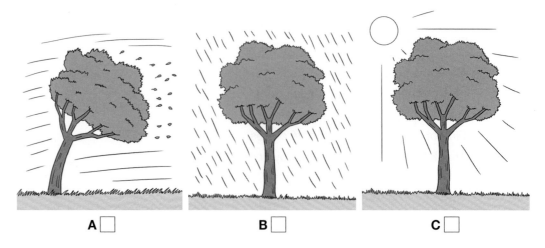

A ☐   B ☐   C ☐

3 Which of these paintings is in the art students' show?

A ☐

B ☐

C ☐

4 What kind of business does the boy's mother have?

A ☐

B ☐

C ☐

5 Where is the café?

PLAN

| Car Park | Café | Lifts | Book Shop |

A ☐

PLAN

| Car Park | Lifts | Café | Book Shop |

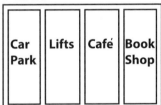

B ☐

PLAN

| Car Park | Book Shop | Lifts | Café |

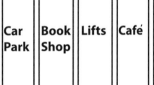

C ☐

6 What are students not allowed to do in the classroom?

A ☐

B ☐

C ☐

Section 1

7 What is bigger at the cinema now?

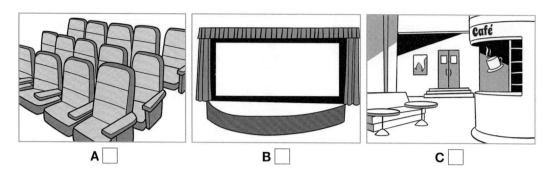

A ☐ B ☐ C ☐

8 Where did they plant the trees?

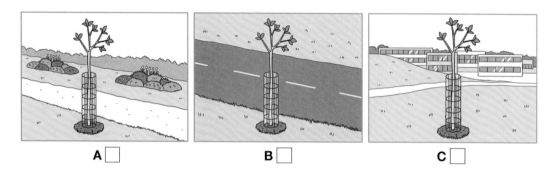

A ☐ B ☐ C ☐

9 How did the man feel when he watched the play?

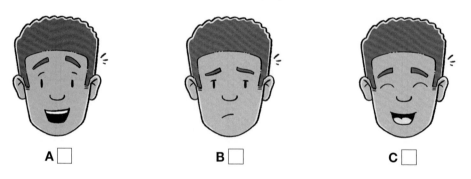

A ☐ B ☐ C ☐

10 What do the players need to do?

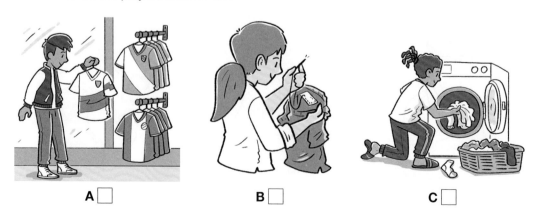

A ☐ B ☐ C ☐

Question 11

▶ You will hear a recording about a printer. Listen to the whole recording once. Then you will hear the recording again with pauses for you to write down what you hear. Make sure you spell the words correctly.

Section 3

Questions 12–16

▶ You will hear a conversation. First, read the notes below. Then listen and complete the sentences with information from the conversation. You will hear the recording twice.

Example The best beach near the hotel is ....*Summer*............ Beach.

12   The beach has nice sand and lots of ....

13   It takes .... minutes to walk to the beach.

14   There are two cafés at the .... end of the beach.

15   Boat trips go from the beach to .... Island.

16   The phone number of the boat trip company is 0768 ....

Section 3

Questions 17–21

▶ You will hear a teacher talking about singing classes. First, read the notes below. Then listen and complete the notes with information from the teacher. You will hear the recording twice.

Example Name of singing teacher: Maria .... *Street* ....

17   Students in Wednesday classes: .... only

18   Students in Thursday classes: .... level

19   Cost of ten lessons: £.. (booked before 30th September)

20   Video online: a .... with Maria's students

21   Email address: Maria@..com

Section 4

Questions 22–26

Read each text and put a cross ☒ by the missing word or phrase, as in the example.

Example

> Because of sound problems at the theatre, tonight's concert is .... If you've already bought tickets online, please click here to get your money back.

A ☐ booked

B ☒ cancelled

C ☐ changed

22

> ## Our end-of-season online .... finish soon!
> ### Don't miss:
> 50% off coats
> 40% off books (50% off for students)
> Ending 14 Jan.

A ☐ gifts

B ☐ clothes

C ☐ sales

23

> Rob,
>
> Thanks for feeding my .... while I'm away. The food's in the cupboard. Joey doesn't do much because he's just hurt his wing.
>
> Jon

A ☐ bird

B ☐ mouse

C ☐ dog

24

The .... is locked at all times so visitors should ring the bell to be let into the building.

A ☐ entrance

B ☐ garage

C ☐ cupboard

25

Summer Party

Enjoy great films which we'll show on a big .... by the lake. Bring sun cream and a jumper because the weather might change!

A ☐ theatre

B ☐ screen

C ☐ picture

26

Mayfield Airport

Please put your phone and computer into the box for staff to check. You will get them back after .... the gate.

A ☐ passing through

B ☐ taking off

C ☐ picking up

Section 5

Questions 27–31

For each question, put a cross ☒ in the box below the correct picture, as in the example.

Example

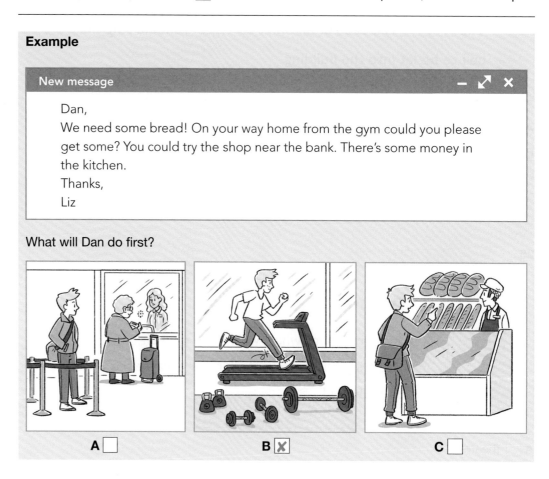

27 Which picture shows the correct rule at the National Park?

National Park
Tours can be booked at the Visitor Centre.
Our guides will show you where to take the best photos!
Please stay on the visitor routes at all times.
No swimming in the river.
Put all rubbish in the bins after eating.

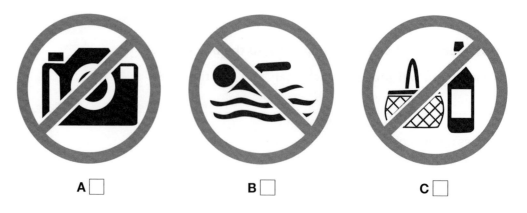

A ☐   B ☐   C ☐

Section 5

28 Which career did most students want to have?

> We asked students about their career plans. The students who
> planned to work in business hoped to earn lots of money. Some
> students wanted to be teachers to help people. The industry
> which interested the highest number of students was computer
> technology, where most students wanted to be engineers.

A ☐   B ☐   C ☐

29 Which business is going to close?

> After thirty years in the city, Zadie's will shut next week. The
> business wasn't doing very well because more people buy
> clothes online now. Many other city centre businesses have
> also closed. Two months ago, Ellie's restaurant was closed
> and turned into an office.

A ☐   B ☐   C ☐

Section 5

30   Which activity is best for people who want to relax?

> After a long, hard day, sitting in front of the TV can make us even more tired. Exercising in the gym can give us more energy. But when you just need to forget your stress and relax, there's nothing better than a long walk outside.

A ☐   B ☐   C ☐

31   Which picture shows a problem that the writer's school is trying to stop?

> # Protecting nature
>
> There are many ways to protect the environment. For example, taking a bus is better than travelling by car. My school doesn't use plastic bottles because they often go into the sea. Companies shouldn't cut down trees because they're more important than new buildings!

A ☐   B ☐   C ☐

Questions 32–35

Read the leaflet below and answer the questions.

Fenstowe is often forgotten by visitors who want to go to the coast or enjoy the shops in Blakesfield, but it is the area's capital of art. Don't miss it!

Our tour begins in the Phillips Centre. This was once a shoe factory and now shows international art. We'll then visit the local art market. There's 10 percent off all photos for our tour group. We'll also meet Bob Danson, an artist who makes beautiful things out of wood. They're amazing!

Example Where do most tourists go shopping?

Blakesfield

32 What is Fenstowe famous for?

....

33 What was the Phillips Centre in the past?

....

34 What costs less for people who are taking the tour?

....

35 What does Bob Danson use to make the things he sells?

....

Section 6

Read the college magazine article below and answer the questions.

Dr Mary Woolton is visiting our college to give a talk on careers in science. She is the country's most famous scientist, and her work on human biology has helped doctors a lot. All her ten books have been translated into thirty languages!

Science students must be at this event. Local people are also welcome, and tickets cost £5. This money goes to Dr Woolton's organisation which helps science students who don't have enough money to continue their education.

Example What will the school's guest talk about?

.... *careers in science* ....

36 What is Dr Woolton's area of science?

....

37 How many books has Dr Woolton written?

....

38 Who has to go to the presentation?

....

39 What does the organisation help people to do?

....

Section 7

Questions 40–46

Read the blog post and complete the notes. Write **no more than three words** from the blog post in each gap.

Evelyn James' Food Blog

Every year, there's an international food festival I love going to. Last year, it was in City Hall but now it's at Market Square. A few years ago, the festival was over a weekend but now it's on for a whole week.

It's a popular festival so I never drive there because the car park is small. Instead, I catch the bus which stops opposite the entrance.

The thing I like doing most at the festival is trying different kinds of food. This year, I ate a wonderful rice and beef dish and then had some fish soup. This was fantastic … even better than the first dish! I'm afraid I spent too much on French cheese, so couldn't buy any Belgian chocolate to take home!

I tried to join a bread-making class, but it was full, so I learned how to make pasta instead.

I also entered a competition and won a cookbook!

Example Type of festival: ....*international food festival*..........

40 This year's festival is at: ....

41 How long the festival is this year: ....

42 Best way to travel to the festival: ....

43 Evelyn's favourite dish: ....

44 Evelyn bought: ....

45 She did a class about: making ....

46 Her prize: ....

Section 8

Question 47

Use the information in **Section 7** to help you write your answer.

You have read the blog post about an international food festival. Now write an email to your friend about food. Write **50–70 words** and include the following information:

- Describe your favourite dish from your country.
- Explain when people eat this dish.
- Say why you like reading food blogs.

Question 48

Choose **one** of the topics below and write your answer in **80–100 words**.

Either:

A Boats

Last weekend, you went on a boat trip with a friend. Look at the pictures and write a description of what happened for your diary.

Or:

B Winter

You and your friends had a fantastic time last winter. Look at the pictures and write a story about it.

Put a cross ☒ in the box next to the task you have chosen.

A ☐   B ☐

Section 10 (1.5 minutes)

Personal information

Examiner:
Now, I'd like you to speak on your own for about 1 minute.

In the test, the examiner might ask you about any different topics. Here are four examples of topics they could ask you about.

TOPIC 1: Friends

Question 1
- **When do you usually spend time with your friends?**

Question 2
- **Can you tell me about your friends?**

Extra questions
- What do you like doing with your friends?
- What sort of places can friends go with each other?
- How do you usually contact your friends?
- Do you have a best friend? Tell me about them.

TOPIC 2: Computers

Question 1
- **How often do you use a computer?**

Question 2
- **What do you use a computer for?**

Extra questions
- How old were you when you started using a computer?
- Is the internet useful for your work or studies? Why/Why not?
- What is your favourite website?
- Do you take a computer on holiday with you?

TOPIC 3: Spending time outside

Question 1
- **How much of your free time do you spend outside?**

Question 2
- **What do you like doing outside?**

Extra questions
- Where can people go for walks where you live?
- Who do you spend time outside with?
- What did you do last time you spent time outside?
- Would you like to go on a really long walk?

TOPIC 4: Television

Question 1
- **Do you enjoy watching TV?**

Question 2
- **How often do you watch TV?**

Extra questions
- What's your favourite TV programme?
- Which room do you watch TV in?
- Do you like to watch TV with other people?
- Do you like TV advertisements?

Section 12A (2 minutes)

Picture

Examiner:

Now, here is a picture of some people in a public place. Please tell me what you can see and what is happening in the picture.

(*Turn to page 159 for your picture.*)

Alright? Begin now please.

 about 1 minute

The examiner might ask you more questions to help you talk about the picture.

> **Extra questions:**
> - Where are the people?
> - How many people can you see?
> - What are the women wearing?
> - What are the women doing?
> - What can you see on the walls?
>
>  *about 1 minute*

Section 12B (2 minutes)

Picture

Examiner:

Now, here is a picture of people at the beach. Please tell me what you can see and what is happening in the picture.

(*Turn to page 159 for your picture.*)

Alright? Begin now please.

 about 1 minute

The examiner might ask you more questions to help you talk about the picture.

> **Extra questions:**
> - Where are the people?
> - What are the boys doing?
> - What are the girls wearing?
> - What's the weather like?
> - Why are the people waiting?
>
> *about 1 minute*

Section 13A (1.5 minutes)

Examiner:

Now, we are going to take part in a role play. Here is a card with the situation on it.
Please read it to yourself.

🕐 *about 15 seconds*

Now let's begin.

> **Test taker's card**
> You want to start an art class. The examiner is the manager of the art school.
>
> • Greet the manager and say what you want to do.
> • Say which day you want to attend.
> • Ask when you pay for the class.
> • Find out what you need to bring.
> • Thank the manager and say goodbye.

(Turn to page 154 for examiner's card.)

Section 13B (1.5 minutes)

Examiner:

Now, we are going to take part in a role play. Here is a card with the situation on it.
Please read it to yourself.

🕐 *about 15 seconds*

Now let's begin.

> **Test taker's card**
> You want to catch the bus to the beach. The examiner is the manager in the
> transport office.
>
> • Greet the manager and explain where you want to go.
> • Tell the manager what time you want to go.
> • Ask where the bus leaves from.
> • Ask about the last bus back.
> • Thank the manager and say goodbye.

(Turn to page 154 for examiner's card.)

GRAMMAR BANK

There is/are

Positive

singular	plural
There's (There is) a/an ...	There are two/some ...

Negative

singular	plural
There isn't a/an ...	There aren't two/any ...

Questions

singular	plural
Is there a/an ... ?	Are there any ... ?

Short answers

singular	plural
Yes, there is./No, there isn't.	Yes, there are./No, there aren't.

Practice

1 Complete the short answers.

a **A:** Is there a pen in your bag?
  B: Yes, ...

b **A:** Are there three girls in the group?
  B: Yes, ...

c **A:** Is there a clock on the wall?
  B: No, ...

d **A:** Are there ten chairs in the classroom?
  B: Yes, ...

2 Complete the sentences with *there is* or *there are*.

a .... a dog on the sofa.

b .... some blue pens in the box.

c .... two sisters in the family.

d .... a picture on the page.

3 Complete the description of Jack's room.

I like my room. There **(a)** .... a bed and there **(b)** .... a small table. There **(c)** .... two big cupboards. There **(d)** .... lots of things inside the cupboards. There **(e)** .... a clock on the table.

There **(f)** .... three posters on my wall. There **(g)** .... a bin on the floor. There **(h)** .... also lots of clothes on the floor.

Countable and uncountable nouns: *some* and *any*

Positive: *some*

countable	uncountable
There are **some shoes** on the floor.	There's **some money** in my purse.

Negtive: *any*

countable	uncountable
There aren't **any** pens.	There isn't **any** milk.

Questions: *some*

countable	uncountable
Are there **any** cups?	Is there **any** music?

We use *some/any*:

- with plural countable nouns.
  some pens
- with uncountable nouns.
  some water

Practice

1 Are these nouns countable (C) or uncountable (U)?

a water   ....

b shelf   ....

c music   ....

d money   ....

e address   ....

f uncle   ....

g sugar   ....

2 Choose the correct words to complete the sentences.

a I have *some / any* money in my bag.

b Harriet has *some / any* interesting photos.

c I don't have *some / any* curtains in my bedroom.

d My grandad doesn't have *some / any* music on his phone.

e We have *some / any* free time today.

3 Complete the conversation with *some* or *any*.

H = Hannah   O = Oliver

H: Do you have **(a)** .... food, Oliver?

O: Yes, there are **(b)** .... bananas in the bowl.

H: Oh. Have you got **(c)** .... chocolate?

O: No, sorry. There is **(d)** .... cake in the kitchen.

H: Have you got **(e)** .... chocolate cake?

O: No, Hannah. There isn't **(f)** .... chocolate in the house!

The definite article: *the*

We can use *the* before a noun to talk about a specific person, thing or situation.

The hotel manager was very nice.

*James' house is **the house on the corner**.*

Practice

1 Put *the* in the correct place in the sentence.
   a I love Brazilian people we met yesterday.
   b Who is boy you sit next to in class?
   c Dad, I need to use car.
   d Moon is very bright tonight.
   e When is test?

Prepositions

For time, we can use:
- *on* for days
  *I am going on holiday **on Friday**.*
- *at* for specific times
  *I will be there **at half past six**.*
- *in* for months and seasons
  *My birthday is **in December**.*
  ***In summer**, I like to have a lot of barbecues.*

For place, we can use many different prepositions such as *next to, in front of, under, behind* and *opposite*.

*My house is **next to** the hospital.*

*The cat is **under** the chair.*

For movement, we can use prepositions such as *in, out, off, up, down, to,* and *from*.

*Can you come **down** from upstairs please?*

*I go **to** school by bus.*

Practice

1 Complete the sentences with the correct preposition.

at   down   in   in   on   up

   a I'll meet you .... 4 o'clock.
   b What do you do with your friends .... summer?
   c I'm going on holiday .... February.
   d I get .... the bus right outside my house.
   e Her office is .... the stairs and on the right.
   f You have to go .... the escalator to get on the underground.

Present simple

Positive

I/We/You/They	dance.
He/She/It	dances.

Negative

I/We/You/They	**don't** dance.
He/She/It	**doesn't** dance.

Questions

Do	I/we/you/they	dance?
Does	he/she/it	dance?

Short answers

Yes,	I/we/you/they	**do.**
	he/she/it	**does.**
No,	I/we/you/they	**don't.**
	he/she/it	**doesn't.**

We use the present simple to talk about:
- something that is always or usually true.
  *She **lives** in the USA.*
- a habit or routine.
  *He **plays** baseball every Saturday.*

1 **Complete the conversation with the present simple form of the verbs in brackets.**

T = Tim   O = Oliver

T: What **(a)** .... you .... (do) at the weekend?

O: I **(b)** .... (like) reading and painting.

T: **(c)** .... your sister .... (play) cards?

O: No, she doesn't. She **(d)** .... (not like) cards.

T: What **(e)** .... your sister .... (do) at the weekend?

O: She **(f)** .... (bake) cookies all the time.

2 **Complete the text with the present simple form of these verbs.**

go (x2)   listen (x2)   not buy   not sound   spend

Anna usually **(a)** .... her free time with her friends. They sometimes **(b)** .... to the cinema on Fridays. On Saturday mornings she always **(c)** .... to town with her friends. Anna **(d)** .... usually .... anything! In the afternoon Anna and her friends often **(e)** .... to music in her bedroom. They **(f)** .... singing their favourite songs, but they **(g)** .... very good!

Adverbs of frequency

always   100%
usually
often
sometimes
not often
not usually
never   0%

Adverbs of frequency come:

- before the main verb.
  He **usually walks** his dog in the morning.

- after the verb *be*.
  She **is always** nervous before exams.

1 **Choose the correct words to complete the sentences.**

a My dad doesn't like films. He *doesn't often go / usually goes* to the cinema.

b Toby *never / always* plays his drums after eleven o'clock at night because everyone is asleep.

c Matt and David *always / sometimes* watch comedy films, but not all the time.

d My family *usually / don't often* go camping in the summer. We love being outside.

2 **Rewrite the sentences. Put the adverbs in brackets in the correct place.**

a We watch films in the morning. (never)

b They aren't late. (usually)

c My mum sings in the car. (often)

d Basketball club is on a Friday. (always)

e Daria doesn't go shopping. (often)

Much/many

We use *much* with uncountable nouns.

*How **much** money does she have?*

*They didn't have **much** time left to plan the party.*

We use *many* with countable nouns.

*How **many** students go to book club?*

*She doesn't have **many** friends.*

1 **Complete the questions with *much* or *many*.**

a How .... clubs do you go to?

b How .... music do you listen to?

c How .... girls are in your class?

d How .... time do you spend playing video games?

e How .... times a year do you go to the cinema?

Present continuous

Positive

I	'm	
He/She/It	's	listening
We/You/They	're	

Negative

I	'm not	
He/She/It	isn't	listening
We/You/They	aren't	

Questions

Am	I	
Is	he/she/it	listening
Are	we/you/they	

Short answers

	I	am.
Yes,	he/she/it	is.
	we/you/they	are.
	I	'm not.
No,	he/she/it	isn't.
	we/you/they	aren't.

We use the present continuous to talk about:

* something happening now.
  Wait a minute. I'm messaging my friend.
  I'm not doing anything at the moment.
  What are you doing right now?

* temporary situations.
  I'm teaching this class because Mr. Hall is on holiday.
  Becky isn't coming football today because she's ill.
  What book are you reading in your English class at the moment?

We often use the present continuous with these time phrases: *right now, at the moment, now, today.*

Remember the spelling rules for verbs + *-ing*:

most verbs	add *-ing*	*walk – walking*
verbs ending in *-e*	remove the final *-e*	*take – taking*
verbs ending in *-ie*	change *-ie* to *-y*	*lie – lying*
verbs ending in one vowel and one consonant	double the final consonant*	*hit – hitting*

*Exceptions include *open – opening*, where the stress is on the first syllable.

Practice

1 **Complete the short answers.**

a **A:** Are you doing your homework?

   B: No, I .... I'm just looking online.

b **A:** Is Ewan playing video games?

   B: Yes, he .... He's playing online.

c **A:** Are you texting your brother?

   B: Yes, I .... He's late!

d **A:** Is Amy using my headphones again?

   B: No, she .... She's using my headphones.

e **A:** Are they chatting online?

   B: Yes, they .... They're talking to their friends in Germany.

2 **Complete the sentences with the present continuous form of the verbs in brackets.**

a At the moment we .... (learn) how to make an app.

b The class .... (not listen) to the teacher.

c Anna .... (show) her friends her favourite vlog.

d We .... (build) a robot. Do you want to watch?

e I .... (not feel) very well. Can you text my dad?

3 **Make sentences in the present continuous to complete the conversation.**

A = Alex   Z = Zara

A: Hi, Zara. **(a)** .... (you / enjoy / computer club)?

Z: Hi, Alex. Yes, I love it! **(b)** .... (we / learn / so many new things)!

A: What **(c)** .... (you / do / at the moment)?

Z: Our teacher **(d)** .... (show / us / how to make a vlog). It's really cool.

A: What kind of vlog?

Z: Well, **(e)** .... (I / make / a vlog about animals), but other people are doing different ones. Dan **(f)** .... (do / a sports vlog).

Present simple and Present continuous

We use the present simple for a regular activity.

She usually leaves the house at 7.30 a.m.

And we use the present continuous for now, today, around this time or for temporary situations.

Today she's leaving the house at 7.00 a.m.

Practice

1 **Choose the correct words to complete the sentences.**

   a Can you use the laptop in a minute? I *'m writing / write* an email.

   b I *'m getting / get* a new phone every year.

   c Every time you *'re clicking / click* on this link, an advert comes on the screen.

   d Can you be quiet? I *'m watching / watch* a film on my laptop.

   e Smile and say 'Cheese!' I *'m taking / take* a selfie!

   f *I'm usually checking / I usually check* my phone when I wake up.

2 **Complete the questions with the present simple or present continuous form of the verbs in brackets.**

   a How many messages .... you .... (send) every day on your phone?

   b I can hear a noise. .... your phone .... (ring)?

   c Which website .... you .... (visit) the most?

   d .... Harry .... (play) video games at the moment?

   e What apps .... you often .... (use)?

3 **Complete the email with the present simple or present continuous form of these verbs.**

be	enjoy	have	rain	stand	stay
visit					

New Message

Hi!

(a) .... you .... a good time on holiday? I **(b)** .... my trip to Spain. The weather **(c)** .... great here – I'm sure it **(d)** .... in the UK right now! The hotel we **(e)** .... in is really cool. Today we **(f)** .... the National Museum of Science and Technology in Madrid. I **(g)** .... in front of it right now. It looks awesome!

Present simple questions: *how*

We can use *how* as a question word to ask many different types of questions.

We can use:

- *How* + adjective to ask for general information.
  How tall are you?

- *How* + *often* + auxiliary verb to ask about frequency.
  How often do you go on holiday?

- *How* + *much/many* for countable or uncountable nouns.
  How much money is left?
  How many people are coming?

- *How* + *long* + auxiliary verb to ask about time.
  How long is the lesson?

- *How* + auxiliary verb for general questions.
  How is your sister?

Practice

1 **Choose the correct question words from the box to complete the questions.**

How	How big	How long	How many
How much	How often		

   a .... is your friend Beth? I haven't seen her for a long time.

   b .... is this T-shirt? I'm not sure it's my size.

   c .... do you see Isabella?

d .... is the flight from here to Paris?

e .... is this bottle of water, please?

f .... books do you have?

Past simple

to be

Positive

I/He/She/It	**was**	hungry.
We/You/They	**were**	at home.

Negative

I/He/She/It	**wasn't**	hungry.
We/You/They	**weren't**	at home.

Practice

1   Choose the correct words to complete the sentences.

My first day at secondary school **(a)** *was / were* really good. The other students **(b)** *was / were* very helpful, so I **(c)** *was / wasn't* nervous at all. I enjoyed the lessons because they **(d)** *were / weren't* boring the teacher **(e)** *was / wasn't* very funny. He made me laugh. What about you? **(f)** *Was / Were* the lessons fun on your first day?

Regular verbs

Regular verbs end in *-ed*. Sometimes the spelling changes.

*arrive – arriv**ed**   study – stud**ied**   talk – talk**ed**
travel – trave**lled***

Positive

I/He/She/It/We/You/They	help**ed**.

Negative

I/He/She/It/We/You/They	**didn't help**.

Irregular verbs

Some verbs have a different form in the past simple.

*be – was   buy – bought   come – came   eat – ate
find – found   go – went   have – had   know – knew
meet – met   read – read   see – saw   win – won*

Positive

I/He/She/It/We/You/They	**went**	to work.

Negative

I/He/She/It/We/You/They	**didn't go**	to work.

We use the past simple to talk about actions that started and finished in the past.

*Jack **helped** Elsa with her homework*

Time expressions with the past simple

We often use these time expressions when we talk about the past: *yesterday, last week, last year, two weeks ago, a month ago, in 2016*.

A: *When did you see Sam?*

B: *I saw him yesterday.*

Practice

1   Complete the sentences with these verbs.

read   talked   took   were   won

a Josh and Alicia .... tired after school.

b I .... an interesting book on holiday.

c The teacher .... to the students about the exam.

d We .... some funny photos at lunch time.

e She .... a prize for her poem.

2   Complete the sentences with the past simple form of the verbs in brackets.

a Last year I .... (travel) to Paris with my history class.

b The biology exam .... (start) at 9 a.m. and .... (finish) at 11 a.m.

c I .... (not study) last night because I .... (not feel) well.

d We .... (run) to school this morning because we .... (be) late.

e The teacher .... (give) us homework.

Past simple questions and short answers

to be

Yes/no questions

Was	I/he/she/it	hungry?
Were	we/you/they	at home?

Short answers

Yes,	I/he/she/it	was.
	we/you/they	were.
No,	I/he/she/it	wasn't.
	we/you/they	weren't.

Wh- questions

Where	was	I/he/she/it?
	were	we/you/they?

Regular and irregular verbs

Yes/no questions

Did	I/he/she/it/we/you/they	help? go?

Short answers

Yes,	I/he/she/it/we/you/they	did.
No,		didn't.

Wh- questions

Who **did**	I/he/she/it/we/you/they	help?
Where **did**		go?

Practice

1 Put the words in the correct order to make questions.

a like / you / primary school / did / your?

b two hours ago / where / you / were?

c finish / the / you / last exercise / did?

d this morning / did / arrive late / you?

2 Complete the questions. Write one word in each gap.

a .... did you go?

b .... it rain?

c .... you happy?

d .... the school trip fun?

Comparative and superlative adjectives

Yes/no questions

type	comparative	superlative
short adjectives *cheap, old, young*	add *-er* *cheaper, older, younger*	add *-est* *the cheapest, the oldest, the youngest*
adjectives ending in *-e* *nice, wide*	add *-r* *nicer, wider*	add *-st* *the nicest, the widest*
one-syllable adjectives ending in one vowel and one consonant *fat, big*	double the final consonant, add *-er* *fatter, bigger*	double the final consonant, add *-est* *the fattest, the biggest*
two-syllable adjectives ending in *-y* *easy, happy*	delete *-y*, add *-ier* *easier, happier*	delete *-y*, add *-iest* *the easiest, the happiest*
long adjectives *interesting*	more/less + adjective *more interesting*	*the most/least* + adjective *the most interesting*
irregular adjectives *good, bad, far*	*better, worse, farther/further*	*the best, the worst, the farthest/the furthest*

Note: The comparative of *fun* is *more fun*.

Comparative adjectives

We use comparative adjectives + *than* to compare two people or things.

*Your jacket is **nicer than** mine.*

*The new teacher is **more interesting than** the last one.*

*The food is **better** here **than** in the other restaurant.*

Sometimes *than* isn't necessary.

*The shops are always **busier** in the summer holidays.*

Practice

1 **Write the comparative form of the adjectives.**

a large ....

b sunny ....

c beautiful ....

d fat ....

e long ....

f difficult ....

g wet ....

2 **Complete the sentences with the comparative form of the adjectives in brackets.**

a The town centre is always .... (quiet) on Sundays.

b The flowers in the park are .... (pretty) than last spring.

c I'm .... (old) than my brother, but he's .... (tall) than me.

d The shops are .... (crowded) in the summer holidays.

e My bag is .... (light) without all those school books!

3 **Complete the article with the comparative form of the adjectives in brackets. Use *than* where necessary.**

> **Where do you like to shop?**
> Shopping in the city is **(a)** .... (fun) shopping in a small town. It's also **(b)** .... (easy) to get to the shops because there are a lot of buses and trains. City shops are **(c)** .... (big), so you can sometimes spend a long time in one shop. The mobile phone shops in the city are **(d)** .... (interesting) the local shops.

Superlative adjectives

We use superlative adjectives to compare one thing or person to others in a group. We use *the* before the superlative adjective.

*I'm **the youngest** student.*

*He's **the nicest** person.*

*We always choose **the biggest** pizza.*

*Matt tells **the funniest** jokes.*

*She bought **the most expensive** shoes.*

*This is **the best** view.*

We often use certain expressions after superlative adjectives: in the world, in the class, in the town.

*The best park **in the town**.*

*The hottest country **in the world**.*

Practice

1 **Write the superlative form of the adjectives.**

a noisy ....

b bad ....

c strange ....

d careful ....

e short ....

f popular ....

g happy ....

2 **Complete the sentences with these superlative adjectives.**

> the fattest   the lowest
> the most comfortable   the quietest
> the sunniest

a You get .... prices when there's a sale.

b Saturday morning is .... time in the shop before lots of customers arrive.

c This is .... chair in the shop. Can we get it for the living room?

d It's .... day of the year and I'm too ill to go out!

e Our cat is .... cat in the street. It's eating too much.

Past continuous

Positive

I/He/She/It	was	talk**ing**.
We/You/They	were	

Negative

I/He/She/It	**wasn't**	
We/You/They	**weren't**	talk**ing**.

Questions

Was	I/he/she/it	
Were	we/you/they	talk**ing**?

Short answers

Yes,	I/he/she/it	**was.**
	we/you/they	**were.**
No,	I/he/she/it	**wasn't.**
	we/you/they	**weren't.**

We use the past continuous:

* for actions happening at a particular time in the past.
  *He **was doing** his homework late last night.*
  *She **wasn't reading** her book this morning.*
  *What **were** you **doing** yesterday morning?*

* to set the scene in a story.
  *It was a cold evening and it **was raining** heavily.*

* We often use the past continuous with time phrases like *yesterday, last weekend, at three o'clock, at half past four, at lunchtime,* etc.
  *Mum was working **at half past three**.*

Practice

1 Complete the sentences with *was, were, wasn't* or *weren't*.

   a Katia .... watching the theatre show.

   b What .... you doing at 8 p.m?

   c It .... raining yesterday – it was really sunny.

   d Why .... Jake laughing?

   e They .... studying. They were watching a concert.

2 Complete the conversation with the past continuous form of the verbs in brackets.

   H = Harriet   F = Finn

   H: Hi, Finn. I didn't see you at the cinema yesterday. What **(a)** .... you ....? (do)

   F: I **(b)** .... (play) football. We have a match soon, so we **(c)** .... (have) extra practice.

H: Oh, right. Well, the cinema was a bit of a disaster! We **(d)** .... (watch) the film and suddenly everything went black!

F: Oh no! Was there no electricity?

H: No, it **(e)** .... (not work) at all. Lots of people **(f)** .... (complain).

F: I hope you **(g)** .... (not watch) a horror film!

Be going to

Positive

I/He/She/It	**is**	
We/You/They	**are**	**going to stay.**

Negative

I/He/She/It	**isn't**	
We/You/They	**aren't**	**going to stay.**

Questions

Is	I/he/she/it	
Are	we/you/they	**going to stay?**

Short answers

Yes,	I/he/she/it	**is.**
	we/you/they	**are.**
No,	I/he/she/it	**isn't.**
	we/you/they	**aren't.**

We use *be going to* to talk about intentions or things we have decided to do.

*I'm **going to stay** with my grandparents next year.*

A: *Are you **going to** talk to him?*
B: *Yes, I **am**.*

Practice

1 Put the words in the correct order to make sentences.

   a to / around the lake / going / we're / ride

   b is / Eliza / to / a helicopter / fly / going

   c get / aren't / you / to / the train / going

   d on the ship / to / they / going / sleep / are

   e Jack / wait / is / to / going / on the platform?

2 Complete the questions with *be going to* and the verbs in brackets. Then complete the short answers.

   a **A:** Is Luke _____ (buy) a train ticket?

      B: Yes, _____ .

   b **A:** Are Issy and Alexa _____ (travel) together?

      B: No, _____ .

   c **A:** Are we _____ (arrive) late?

      B: Yes, _____ .

   d **A:** _____ your sister _____ (get) the train, too?

      B: No, _____ .

   e **A:** Are you both _____ (wait) outside?

      B: Yes, _____ .

Will

Positive

I/He/She/It/We/You/They	will	win.

Negative

I/He/She/It/We/You/They	won't	win.

Questions

Will	I/he/she/it/we/you/they	win?

Short answers

Yes,	I/he/she/it/we/you/they	will.
No,	I/he/she/it/we/you/they	won't.

We use *will* or *won't* (*will not*) to talk about predictions or things we think or know will happen.

It **won't be** very busy at the shopping centre.

A: **Will** it be hot in Portugal?

B: Yes, it **will**.

We often use *I think/I don't think* before *will*.
I think she**'ll come** later.

Note the short forms we use with *I/you/he/she/we/they*.

I **will** – *I'll*   *she* **will** – *she'll*   *we* **will** – *we'll*

1 Complete the sentences with *will/'ll* or *won't* and the verbs in brackets.

   a We _____ (go) on the underground because it's faster.

   b I think they _____ (sail) around Europe next year.

   c The bus _____ (not come) today because it's snowing.

   d _____ you _____ (write) to me from China?

2 Complete the conversations. Use *be going to* or *will* and the verbs in brackets.

   a **A:** The car park is full. What _____ we _____ (do)?

      B: There's another one near the station. I think it _____ (have) spaces.

   b **A:** I _____ (meet) Charlie at the train station. Do you want to come?

      B: Sorry, I can't. I _____ (visit) my grandma.

Present continuous for future

We use the present continuous to talk about definite plans or arrangements for the near future.

I'm taking my bike to the beach later.

Are you coming to the cinema?

We often use these future time phrases with the present continuous: *this afternoon, later, tonight, tomorrow, next week, at the weekend, in the summer*.

Note: We don't usually say *going to go*. We use the present continuous.

~~We're going to go to the cinema tonight.~~

We're going to the cinema tonight.

1 Complete the sentences with these verbs.

are riding	is catching	'm getting
'm meeting	're taking	're travelling

   a We _____ around Europe by train this summer.

   b I _____ Alice outside the classroom after the lesson.

c They _____ sandwiches on the long car journey.

d My parents _____ their motorbikes to Scotland.

e I _____ the bus to school.

Ability and possibility: *can/could*

Positive

I/He/She/It/We/You/They	can	speak French.
	could	

Negative

I/He/She/It/We/You/They	can't	speak French.
	couldn't	

Questions

Can	I/he/she/it/we/you/they	speak French.
Could		

Short answers

Yes,	I/he/she/it/we/you/they	can.
		could.
No,	I/he/she/it/we/you/they	can't.
		couldn't.

We use *can* + infinitive without *to* talk about ability and possibility in the present.

*I **can play** football, but I'm not very good.*

*Learning to swim **can be** hard.*

We use *could* + infinitive without *to* talk about ability in the past.

*Matt **could swim** when he was four years old.*

Practice

1   **Write short answers.**

A: Can he play table tennis? ✔

B: Yes, he can.

a A: Could you do karate at primary school? ✗
B: No,

b A: Could she do karate at primary school? ✗
B: _____

c A: Could they do karate at primary school? ✔
B: _____

d A: Could he do karate at primary school? ✔
B: _____

2   **Complete the conversations with *can*, *can't*, *could* or *couldn't*.**

a A: _____ we swim on this beach?
B: No, we _____ . The sea _____ be dangerous here.

b A: _____ you play badminton?
B: Yes, I _____, but I only learnt to play this year. I _____ play at all last year.

c A: _____ you walk when you were one?
B: Yes, I _____, but my sister _____ walk until she was one and a half.

Obligation: *have to/had to*

Positive

I/We/You/They	have to	train every day.
	had to	
He/She/It	has to	
	had to	

Negative

I/We/You/They	don't have to	train every day.
	didn't have to	
He/She/It	doesn't have to	
	didn't have to	

We use *have to* + infinitive without *to* talk about general rules in the present or something that is necessary.

*You **have to wear** a helmet when you're biking.*

*He **has to wear** special clothes to play golf.*

We use *had to* + infinitive without *to* talk about general rules in the past or something that was necessary.

*My sister **had to wear** a uniform at school.*

*Camilla **had to drink** a lot of water during the race.*

We use *don't/doesn't have to* (present) and *didn't have to* (past) when there is no obligation.

*You **don't have to** buy a racket. You can use mine.*

*I **didn't have to buy** a racket. I used my friend's.*

Practice

1 **Choose the correct words to complete the sentences.**

a We *had to / have to* stop the tournament yesterday because of bad weather.

b You *have to / don't have to* wear protective clothing, but it's always a good idea.

c We *had to / didn't have to* wear wetsuits because the water wasn't cold.

d Eric *have to / has to* study every day before an important exam.

2 **Complete the sentences with the correct form of *have to*.**

a .... you .... wear a helmet when you ride a bike?

b I .... leave tennis practice early yesterday because I hurt my foot.

c Charlotte .... practise diving every day when she's preparing for a competition.

d You .... bring your own ball. You can borrow one.

Requests and permission: *can, could, would*

We can request, or ask for, something using:

- *can/could* + subject + infinitive without *to*
  Could you pass me the salt, please?

- subject + *would like* + object/infinitive
  I would like a cup of tea, please.
  I would like to see the doctor, please.

We can answer questions with *can* and *could* with:
Yes, *I/you/he/she/it* **can**/**could**.
No, *I* **can't**/**couldn't**.

We can ask for permission with *can* + subject + infinitive without *to*.
Can I stay at Lucy's tonight, Mum?

Practice

1 **Choose the correct word to complete the sentences.**

a *Can / Would* I go to the cinema tonight?

b I *would like / could* a cup of coffee.

c **A:** Can I open the window?
   B: No, you *can / can't*.

Present perfect

Positive

I/We/You/They	have	**been**	to Kenya.
He/She/It	has		

Negative

I/We/You/They	**haven't**	**been**	to Kenya.
He/She/It	**hasn't**		

We use the present perfect (*have/has* + past participle) to talk about experiences in our lives up to now. We do not say when the experience was.

*He's **been** on a safari.* (but we are not saying when)
*They **haven't seen** snow.*

For the past participle of regular verbs, we add *-ed*.
climb – climbed   cook – cooked

Some irregular verbs are the same as the past simple.
put – put – put   read – read – read

Other irregular verbs have a different form.
see – saw – seen   swim – swam – swum
write – wrote – written

Practice

1 **Complete the sentences with *'ve* or *'s* and the past participle of the verbs in brackets.**

a We .... (camp) near the ocean.

b She .... (go) to Korea.

c They .... (see) the film.

d It .... (snow) in the mountains.

2 **Make the sentences in exercise 1 negative.**

a *We haven't camped near the ocean.*

3 **Complete the sentences with *have/has gone* or *have/has been*.**

a Stefano isn't here. He .... to Malaysia.

b This is a beautiful island. .... you .... here before?

c I .... to Cuba. I had a holiday there.

d .... she .... home? She wasn't feeling well on the walk.

4 **Complete the questions with the present perfect form of the verbs in brackets. Then complete the short answers.**

a **A:** .... (you/take) lots of photos of the beautiful beach?
   B: No, I ....

b A: .... (she/enjoy) her holiday?

B: Yes, she ....

c A: .... (they/read) about the weather?

B: Yes, ...

d A: ....(Jo/spend) a night in a tent?

B: No, ...

e A: .... (Ben and Lucy/ride) a camel in the desert?

B: Yes, ...

Present perfect with *ever* and *never*

Positive

Have	I/we/you/they			
		ever	**climbed**	a mountain?
Has	he/she/it			

Negative

I/We/You/They				
	have	**never**	**climbed**	a mountain.
He/She/It				

We use *ever* in questions, to ask if something has happened. There is no specific time.

Have you ever swum in the ocean?
Has he ever been to Australia?

We use n*ever* to say something hasn't happened.
She's never skied in the Alps.
We've never stayed in a tent.

Ever and *never* go between *have/has* and the past participle.
She's never slept under the stars.

The verb *go* has two past participles. Compare:
She's been to Belgium. (She went and she left).
She's gone to Belgium. (She's in Belgium now).

Practice

1 Put the words in the correct order to make sentences.

a she / lost / has / a competition / ever?

b ridden / he / a mountain bike / has / ever?

c you / have / ever / an ice cube / eaten?

d seen / never / they've / tigers

First conditional

If + present tense	will/won't + infinitive without to
If my dad **opens** a café,	**I'll help** him.
If you **eat** lots of sweets now,	you **won't be** hungry at dinner time.

We use the first conditional to talk about possible situations and consequences in the future.

We use a comma when *if* comes at the beginning of the sentence.
If she passes the exam, she'll be very happy.
(situation)   (consequence)

We don't use a comma when *if* comes in the middle of the sentence.
She'll be very happy if she passes the exam.
(situation)   (consequence)

Practice

1 Put the words in the correct order to make sentences. Start with the words in bold.

a stomach ache / too much chocolate, / you'll get / you eat / **if** /

b hungry / your sandwich / if / you don't feel / **I'll eat**

c we won't be / if / late for dinner / we hurry up,

d an award / upset / I don't get / **I won't be** / if

2 Choose the correct words to complete the sentences.

a If *it's / will be* sunny, we'll eat by the river.

b If you *don't follow / won't follow* the instructions, the cake won't taste nice.

c I *buy / 'll buy* you some snacks if you're hungry.

d If Emma *doesn't finish / won't finish* her pizza, she won't get any ice cream.

3 Complete the first conditional sentences. Use the correct form of the verbs in brackets.

a If we .... (start) cooking now, the food .... (be) ready by 7 p.m.

b We .... (have) a picnic if it .... (not rain).

c You ....(be) hungry later if you .... (not have) anything to eat.

d Dad .... (call) me if he .... (need) anything from the supermarket.

Advice: should

Positive

I/He/She/It/We/You/They	**should**	eat healthy food.

Negative

I/He/She/It/We/You/They	**shouldn't**	eat junk food.

Questions

Should	I/he/she/it/we/you/they	eat junk food.

We use *should + infinitive* without *to* to give or ask for advice.

*You **shouldn't eat** a lot of chocolate.*
***Should** I **buy** these trainers?*

Practice

1 Complete the questions with *should* and these verbs.

bake   bring   grill   have

a How long .... I .... the cake for?

b What food .... I .... to the party?

c ....we .... the meat or fry it?

d What time .... we .... dinner?

2 Complete the advice. Use *should* or *shouldn't* and these verbs.

be   eat   drink   find   go   make sure

I want to get fit, but I'm not sure how.

Here's my advice for getting fit. Firstly, I think you **(a)** .... a gym or exercise class you like. It **(b)** .... difficult. Also, you **(c)** ....well – healthy food is really important. You **(d)** .... to fast food restaurants. Instead, you **(e)** .... that you eat lots of fruit and vegetables. Another important thing is water. You **(f)** .... lots of water every day.

SPEAKING ROLE CARDS

Test 1, Section 13A

Examiner's script:

You want to go on a trip on a tour boat. I am the ticket seller for the tour boat. Alright? You start.

> **Suggested prompts**
> * Good morning/afternoon. How can I help?
> * Of course. Do you want to go in the morning or the afternoon?
> * The boat leaves at 2.
> * It's 10 euros per person.
> * Here you are, thank you very much.

Thank you. That is the end of the test.

Test 1, Section 13B

Examiner's script:

You want to buy a present in a book shop. I am the book shop manager. Alright? You start.

> **Suggested prompts**
> * Hello, can I help you?
> * What sort of books does he/she like?
> * Well, I have a lovely book here that he/she might enjoy.
> * It's £15.
> * OK. Thank you. Here you are.

Thank you. That is the end of the test.

Test 2, Section 13A

Examiner's script:

You want to do a tennis class at your local sports centre. I am the sports centre receptionist. Alright? I'll start.

Hello/Good morning/Good afternoon

> Suggested prompts
> - Yes of course. There is a class in the morning or the afternoon. Which would you like?
> - The class is at 3 p.m.
> - An hour and a half. It finishes at 4:30.
> - You can pay when you come to the class.
> - You're welcome.

Thank you. That is the end of the test.

Test 2, Section 13B

Examiner's script:

You are at the cinema to buy tickets. I am the ticket seller. Alright? You start.

> Suggested prompts
> - Hello – how can I help?
> - Yes, there are plenty. How many would you like?
> - OK. And do you want any snacks too?
> - We've got chocolates, ice creams and drinks.
> - OK, here you are. Thanks.

Thank you. That is the end of the test.

Test 3, Section 13A

Examiner's script:

You want to organise a party and want your friend to help. The examiner is your friend. Alright? You start.

> **Suggested prompts**
> * Yes of course – shall I bring some food?
> * OK. When is the party?
> * OK – I'll see you there.
> * Yes of course – what time?
> * You're welcome!

Thank you. That is the end of the test.

Test 3, Section 13B

Examiner's script:

You are meeting your friend in a café but you arrive late and are calling your friend to say you'll be late. I am your friend. Alright? I'll start.

Hello?

> **Suggested prompts**
> * That's OK – what happened?
> * Oh dear! When will you get here?
> * OK, I'll order a coffee wait for you here.
> * Say goodbye.

Thank you. That is the end of the test.

Test 4, Section 13A

Examiner's script:

You are going to your friend Sam's party. I am also going to the party. Alright? I'll start.

Hello/Good morning/Good afternoon

> Suggested prompts
> * Do you know what time Sam's party starts this weekend?
> * Thanks. What are you taking for a present? I'm not sure what to get …
> * Good idea! How are you getting there?
> * It's OK thanks, I'm going with my brother, so I'll see you there! Bye!

Thank you. That is the end of the test.

Test 4, Section 13B

Examiner's script:

You want to catch a train and need some help. I am a station worker. Alright? You start.

> Suggested prompts
> * Can I help you?
> * It goes in 30 minutes.
> * It leaves from platform number 7.
> * There's a ticket office just behind you.
> * It closes at 6 p.m.
> * You're welcome.

Thank you. That is the end of the test.

Test 5, Section 13A

You want to start an art class. I am the manager of the art school. Alright? I'll start.

Hello/Good morning/Good afternoon

> **Suggested prompts**
> - We have classes every day – which would you like?
> - Yes, that's fine. We have places then.
> - You can pay on the first day of the class.
> - Just bring a snack – we provide everything else.
> - Goodbye.

Thank you. That is the end of the test.

Test 5, Section 13B

Examiner's script:
You want to catch a bus to the beach. I am the ticket seller. Alright? I'll start.

Hello/Good morning/Good afternoon

> **Suggested prompts**
> - Of course. We have buses all day.
> - Ok, there's one just after that.
> - You need to go to stop 4, at the bus station entrance.
> - The last one is at 7:45 – don't miss it!
> - You're welcome – goodbye.

Thank you. That is the end of the test.

Section 12A

Section 12B

Section 12A

Section 12B

Section 12A

Section 12B

Section 12A

Section 12B

Section 12A

Section 12B

SPEAKING BANK

Section 10

In this section of the test the examiner will ask you to introduce yourself and then ask you lots of questions. They might ask you questions to make you talk about some of these kinds of topics:

- Activities, routines, places and people in your everyday life
- Describing something you do, did in the past or might do in the future
- Hobbies and pastimes
- Routines
- Things you do or don't do, would like to do or wouldn't like to do
- Travel, holidays and places you have visited
- Your friendships or family
- Your likes, dislikes and reasons why

If you stop talking before the time is finished, the examiner may ask you extra questions to invite you to keep talking.

See Test 1, Section 10, on page 49.

Exam help

✔ When you answer the questions, use the same tense you hear in the examiner's questions. So, for example, if the examiner asks you *How often do you ...?* You need to use the same tense (the present simple) and the right adverb of frequency or frequency expression in your answer.

✔ You could then follow that by saying something about the past with the past simple tense, e.g. how you did something differently in the past: *But when I was a child, I ....* This will show the examiner that you can use more than one different tense correctly.

✔ If the examiner asks: *What would you (really) like to do ...?* You should use the expression *I'd (really) like to ...* in your answer. If the examiner asks a question like *Tell me about ....* You have to choose the correct tense to use yourself: present simple, present continuous, past simple or possibly a future tense.

✔ In all of your answers you need to use vocabulary for the things, people and places in your everyday life and language for giving your opinion, e.g. *I think ... In my opinion ...,* etc.

Useful language

Have you got a ...?
Yes, I have./No, I haven't.
He/She's called .../It's a/an ...
He/She's older/younger than me.
It's big/beautiful/interesting.

How often do you ...?
... every day/once a week/twice a year.

Do you ...?
Yes, I do. I like ...
No, I don't. I don't like ... But when I was younger I ...

Did you ...?
Yes, I ... last year/two years ago ...
No I didn't because I ...

What do you think ...?

Is it good to ...?
I think/believe ... / In my opinion .../
For me, ...

What/Who is your favourite ...?
My favourite ... is ... because ...

What would you really like to do ...?
I'd (really) like to ... because ...

Tell me about ...?
I usually eat/go/have ... I like/
don't like ... because ...

Practice

1 Look at the examiner's questions (a–h). Write whether each question asks you to talk about *everyday life, the past, the future, things a person likes,* or *a person/place/thing*. Sometimes more than one topic will be correct.

a Tell me about the last time you had fun.

.... *the past* ....

b What's your favourite type of music?

....

c Tell me something about your weekend plans.

....

d What is your dream job?

....

e Tell me about your favourite way to travel.

....

f Tell me about your best friend.

....

g What is your morning routine?

....

h What does your room look like?

....

2 Now write a new question for each category.

everyday life

a .... *What is your evening routine?* ....

the past

b ....

the future

c ....

things a person likes

d ....

a person/place/thing

e ....

3 Match the questions with possible follow-up questions you might be asked.

1 Describe a place you've visited.

2 Tell me about a good teacher you've had.

3 What do you think of online classes?

4 What things do you have in your kitchen?

a Did you get a lot of homework?

b How do you ask questions online?

c How long were you there?

d Do you like to cook?

4 Look at questions in exercise 1. Finish the sentences.

a It was last weekend. We went with my friends to …

b I think my favourite type of music is … because …

c At the weekend, I'm going to …

d In the future, I would like to …

e My favourite way of travel is definitely …

f My best friend's name is …

g After I wake up, I like to …

h My room is …

5 Now record yourself answering the questions from 1 and 2. Then listen to your answers. Make notes about other words or phrases you could have used. If your answer was too short, think about follow-up questions you might have been asked. Finally, try recording yourself answering the questions again.

In this section of the test, the examiner will give you a picture to describe. You will have one minute to describe the picture. If you finish before your time is up, the examiner will ask you some more questions.

See Test 1, Section 12, on page 52.

Useful language

Describing the picture

I can see a city, with …
There are two women who are …
They are all listening to …
One of the women/men is wearing
a …
It has some …
On the road there's a …
He/She's going to buy …
They are about to …
In front of the … there's a …
He/She looks like …

Answering questions

How many people can you see?
I can see four people.
Where are they?
They are in the middle of a big city.
What is he/she wearing?
She is wearing a white shirt, black trousers and a hat.
What is he/she doing?
He is running to the bus stop.
What is he/she going to buy?
He is going to buy a bottle of water.

Exam help

✔ When you start speaking, it's helpful to think of and say your answers to the questions the examiner could ask you about the picture. These will be questions that start with words like: *What? How? Where? What is … like?* For example, *What are the children doing? What is the man wearing?*

✔ Remember that you're describing what is happening in the picture. That means you need to use the present continuous tense, e.g. *the children are walking on the beach, the woman is wearing a long coat.* But you will also need to use the present simple tense to say facts about the people in the picture or the place where they are, e.g. *The park is …; The boy has …,* etc.

✔ Use vocabulary for everyday situations and things, such as places, types of people, popular activities. It would also be useful to link the different parts of your description with linking words. You could use words like *then, too, as well* or *also* when you move from describing one thing to describing another thing.

Practice

1 In 30 seconds, make a list of all the things you can see in the picture (e.g. *bike, stairs,* etc.). Compare your list with a partner's.

2 Now, in 30 seconds, make a list of all the actions you can see in the picture (e.g. *talking, holding,* etc.). Compare your list with a partner's.

3 Imagine you are an examiner. Think of three questions you could ask about the picture. Write down your questions. Ask these questions to your partner.

4 Look at the name of the place. Write two things and two actions you might see in a picture of that place. In the final circle, write the name of a place as well as two things and two actions.

5 Choose one of the pictures in Section 12 (12A or 12B) of Test 1 on page 155. Make a list of the following:

a the type of place you see in the picture (e.g. city, farm, village)

b the people you can see in the picture (e.g. two men, one woman)

c the action(s) that one person in the picture is doing

d the types of vehicles you can see in the picture (e.g. car, bus, etc.)

e the buildings you can see in the picture (e.g. shops)

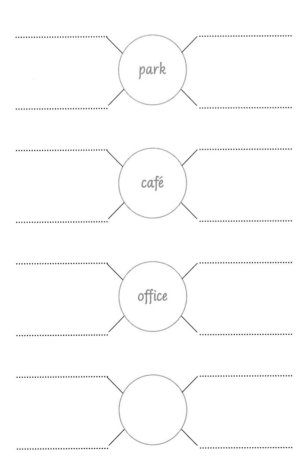

SPEAKING BANK

In this section, you will get a card with a situation on it. Read it carefully and think about your role. The card will tell you who should start the conversation.

See Test 1, Section 13, Task 13A on page 55.

Test taker's card

You want to buy a ticket to go on a trip on a tour boat. The examiner is the ticket seller in the tour boat office.

- Greet the ticket seller.
- Say you want to buy a ticket for the tour boat.
- Find out the time of the afternoon boat.
- Ask about the ticket price.
- Agree to buy the ticket.

Exam help

- ✔ Whatever situation you have on your card, there are some phrases you can always use. For example, greeting the examiner. You can use phrases like *Hello, Good morning, Good afternoon* to do that.
- ✔ You will always have to ask the examiner something or find out some information from the examiner. When you need to ask the examiner something.
- ✔ You may need to make a request, which means using questions like: *Can/Could I …?* if you want to do something, or *Can/Could you …?* if you want the examiner to do something for you. When you need to get some information, you can use the *Wh-* question forms you should be able to use at A2 level such as: *What sorts of books does he like?* or *How long does it take?*
- ✔ You will often have to explain something, like what food someone can bring to a party, so knowing how to use words like *can, might* or *have to* is helpful, e.g. *You can bring sandwiches.* You may also have to say which thing would be right for someone or give advice to the examiner, so knowing how to use words like *might* and *should* or *shouldn't* is helpful, e.g. *Here is a book he might enjoy.*

Useful language

Greeting
Hello
Good morning
Good afternoon

Say what you want
I'd like a …, please.
Can/Could I have a …, please?

Ask the examiner something or for something
What/Where/When/Who/How …?
Can/Could you …, please?
What do you think …?

Give your opinion or give advice
I think …/In my opinion …
You should …

Agree to do something
I'll take that, please.
Let's do that.

Thank the examiner and say goodbye
Thank you (very much)
Goodbye

1 Match the tasks from the situation card in Section 13A of Test 1 on page 150 with the phrases you can use for them.

a Greet the ticket seller.

b Say you want to buy a ticket for the tour boat.

c Find out the time of the boat in the afternoon.

d Ask about the ticket price.

e Agree to buy the ticket.

1 How much does the ticket cost?

2 Good morning

3 I'd like a ticket for the tour boat, please.

4 OK, I'll get that ticket.

5 What time does the afternoon boat leave?

2 Match the tasks from the situation card in Section 13B of Test 1 on page 150 with the phrases you can use for them.

a Greet the manager.

b Say who you want to buy a book for.

c Explain what they like reading about.

d Ask the price of the book.

e Say you'd like to buy it.

1 I'd like to buy a book for a friend.

2 They like reading crime novels.

3 I'll take that, please.

4 Good afternoon.

5 How much does that book cost?

3 Look at the cards. Fill in the blanks with possible instructions.

Card 1

You want to meet your friend for coffee on _____ instead Tuesday. The examiner is your friend.

• Greet your friend
• Tell your friend that you _____ on Tuesday.
• Apologise for cancelling the plan.
• Find out what time your friend is free on _____.
• _____.

Card 2

You are at a crowded theatre with a friend. You see a man sitting alone with empty seats to his left and right. You want him to move. The examiner is the stranger who you want to move.

• _____.

• Find out if the stranger is waiting for a friend.
• Ask the stranger to _____.
• Explain why you want the stranger to _____.
• _____.

---

4 Show your cards from (3) to a partner. Act out the role play with your partner. They should be the test taker and you should be the examiner. Then switch roles and do it again.

HOW TO PREPARE

Speaking sections (Level 1, A2)

The Level 1 Speaking test lasts about 5 minutes and has three sections where you answer questions about personal information, describing a picture and taking part in a role play. If you know what questions to expect and how you should answer them, you will be calmer and more confident during the actual test. It is important to know exactly what each section involves, how long it lasts and what things you can do to prepare for it. Here are some tips for dealing with each section of the Speaking test:

Section 10: Personal information *1.5 minutes*

What happens in this section?

The first section of the Speaking test lasts approximately 1.5 minutes and consists of brief questions about topics of personal information and personal interest. After asking you to say your name, the examiner will ask you another question to establish the topic. He/she will then in invite you to talk for a bit longer on the topic saying, for example, *Tell me something about …* (*the sort of food you eat*). You should speak for as long as you can and after about 30 seconds, the examiner will ask you a few more questions on the same topic. You should try to keep the conversation going until the examiner asks you to stop talking.

How can I prepare for this section?

The best way to prepare for this section is to make a list of topics the examiner might ask you about your life and personal interests: where you live, who you live with/socialise with (friends/family), what your daily routine is like, what sort of food you eat (likes/dislikes), the clothes you like to wear (fashion/shopping), what you do (work/studies), what you like doing in your free time (music/film/ sport, etc.), what sort of holidays you like (travel/transport), etc.

Once you have a list of topics think of as many words as you can that match the topics. If you need more or want to learn more vocabulary look for more words to add.

For more information and vocabulary practice:

 Go to **Vocabulary maps** *on* **Pearson English Portal** *for useful language.*

 Do **Vocabulary activities** *on* **Pearson Practice English** *app for more practice.*

Prepare some questions that you think the examiner might ask you about each topic and think about how you could answer them. Make a list of useful vocabulary and phrases for each topic, practise saying them out loud and check the pronunciation with your teacher. It's a good idea to create a special vocabulary notebook and organise it into different topics so you can keep adding new words and phrases as you learn them.

During the test, listen carefully to the questions the examiner asks you and try to answer them as completely as you can. You need to provide answers that consist of more than a few words so try to think of reasons and/or examples to illustrate the things you are saying. This will give you an opportunity to show the examiner how you can organise your ideas as well as show him/her how much grammar and vocabulary you know.

Section 12: Describing a picture 2 minutes

What happens in this section?

In Section 12 the examiner will give you picture and ask you to talk about it. He/she will usually say something like: *Here is a picture of … Please tell me what you can see in the picture.* Then you should talk for as long as you can about the picture. After that the examiner will ask you some more questions related to the picture and you should try to keep the conversation going until the examiner asks you to stop.

How can I prepare for this section?

The pictures generally show common, everyday scenes and situations. The setting of the picture could be a house (e.g. rooms or the garden), a street, a shop, a restaurant, a café, a park, a school or a workplace. The preparation you do for the previous section of the Speaking test will also help you describe the pictures in Section 12. In addition, you should also make a list of phrases for describing where things are in relation to each other. Prepositions and phrases like *in the foreground* and in *the background* are very useful when you are describing pictures. Finally, it's a good idea to practise common language functions such as describing people, places and activities as much as you can before you take the test.

During the test, try to talk for as long as you can about the picture. Think about what's happening, who the people are, where they are, what they are doing/going to do, what the weather is like, etc. Try to give reasons for the points you are making. For example, you could say: *I think the weather is cold because the people are wearing hats and coats.* Aim to use short, simple sentences with a subject, verb and object rather than unconnected words and try to use a wide range of different vocabulary and expressions. Try not to repeat yourself too much and avoid saying things like *I can see …* too often.

Section 13: Role play 1.5 minutes

What happens in this section?

The final section of the Speaking test consists of a role play between you and the examiner. He/she will give you a role card saying, *Here is a card with a situation on it.* You will have up to 10 seconds to read the card and think about the situation. After this, the examiner will ask if you are ready and he/she will have a conversation with you asking questions and responding to you according to the needs of the situation and the prompts on the role card.

How can I prepare for this section?

The role play generally involves basic social situations such shopping, ordering food and drink, etc. Depending on the situation, you will need to show that you can deal with a variety of language functions: asking for things and/or information, making and responding to requests/offers, accepting/declining invitations, asking for/giving directions, suggesting/responding to suggestions, thanking, apologising, etc.

The best way to prepare for the role play is to make a list of useful phrases that are related to each of the language functions listed above. Again, it would be a good idea to practise saying these out loud and to practise the pronunciation with your teacher. You should make a note of the useful phrases in your vocabulary book and try to memorise them.

During the test, you should use the preparation time to think about ideas, statements or questions based on the information provided on your test card. This will activate the vocabulary you know and stop you from hesitating when it is your turn to speak. Think about the role the examiner is playing as this will affect how you interact with each other. Try to take control of the role play but listen carefully to what the examiner says and how he/she responds. It is fine to ask him/her to repeat a question and/or answer to your question. The important thing with the role play is to achieve the end goal so take your time and try to keep the conversation going as smoothly as you can.

WRITING BANK

Section 8

In this section of the test you either write an email, a letter, a postcard or a note. You need to write between 50 and 70 words. You can use information from Section 7 of the Reading paper but remember to always use your own words.

Email

See Test 1, Section 8, on page 41.

Sample answer

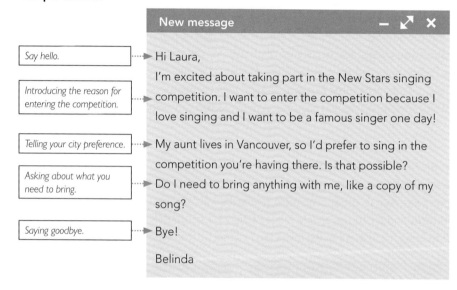

Say hello. → Hi Laura,

Introducing the reason for entering the competition. → I'm excited about taking part in the New Stars singing competition. I want to enter the competition because I love singing and I want to be a famous singer one day!

Telling your city preference. → My aunt lives in Vancouver, so I'd prefer to sing in the competition you're having there. Is that possible?

Asking about what you need to bring. → Do I need to bring anything with me, like a copy of my song?

Saying goodbye. → Bye!

Belinda

Useful language

Emails

Hi/Hello!
How are you?/How is it going?
I'm excited to …
I want to …
What do you think?
Do you want to …?
Can you … for me?
Thank you for inviting/asking me …
Bye!
Write back soon!
Take care!

Informal Letters

Dear Tom,
Thanks for your email!
Thanks for writing to me.
I'm writing about …
Could you/Could I …, please?
I'd prefer to …
I would like to …
Is that possible?
Do I need to …?
Thank you very much for …
I hope to hear from you soon.
Thanks,

Postcards

Hi/Hello …
We're having a great time in …
Yesterday we went/did/had …
Tomorrow we're going to …
I hope everything is OK at home.
See you soon.
Bye!

Notes

Hi/Hello + first name(s)
Can you … /Can I …?
I need …
I want …
Thanks,

Exam help

✔ Go back to Test 1 Section 7 on page 37 and quickly read the text again. This will help you to remember the situation that you're writing about.

✔ Make sure you know which type of text you need to write and remember the useful language for that type of text. Your text needs to include the type of language people usually use in an email, a letter, a postcard or a note. You also need to write about all of the three things listed in the instructions in your text.

✔ Think about how you organise your text on the page.

✔ Remember to start with a friendly greeting (Hi Laura).

✔ Write complete sentences and check that you are using the correct form of verbs (present, past or future).

✔ Don't be afraid to use some interesting vocabulary and expressions you know.

✔ You could start a new line for each of the things you have to write about. This will clearly show the examiner that you added all of these three things.

✔ When you've finished writing, count the number of words in your text.

Practice

1 **Read Laura's answer. Find the places where she:**

 a says hello.

 b gives information about how to enter the competition.

 c gives information about choosing a place to do the competition.

 d ends the text politely.

New message

Hi Belinda,

Thank you for your email. We are so happy that you want to join our competition!

It is still possible to enter in Vancouver. All you need to do is register on our website and complete the form. There is a question about the city you want to choose.

Please bring your own song and be prepared to sing it for us on your competition day.

Hope to see you there!

Laura

---

2 **Match the words a–e with their definitions 1–5. Then write one sentence using each word.**

 a possible

 b register

 c prepared

 d join

 e complete

 1 fill with information

 2 become a part of

 3 it means that you can do it

 4 be ready to

 5 put your name on a list for something

Planning your answer

Starting an email/informal letter

Start by saying *hello* to the person you are writing to. There are different ways to say *hello* in an email and an informal letter.

Next you can ask the person a question (*How are you?*, *How's it going?*) before starting to write about the bullet points in the question.

Then start to write about the first point of the email. Start talking about the topic (using phrases like *I'm writing about …* or *I'm excited to …*).

Middle of the email/letter

Write about the other main points in the question. Try to give as much information as you can. If you don't have much to say about any of the points you need to write about, try to add thoughts, feelings or more description. Think about this part before you start writing it.

Finishing your email/informal letter

Add a comment or question at the end (like *What do you think?* or *Do I need to bring anything?*).

Checklist

When you finish writing your email, use this checklist.

 ● **Content**
   Have you covered all the bullet points?
   Have you used interesting vocabulary and structures?
   Is your message clear?
   Is your email/letter organised correctly?

 ● **Communicative achievement**
   Who are you writing to? Did you write *hello/dear*?
   Is your style correct? (formal/informal)

 ● **Language**
   Are your verb tenses correct?
   Is your spelling and punctuation correct?
   Does your email or letter make sense?

Section 9

In this section of the test you will write a description, a story or a diary entry. You need to write between 80 and 100 words. You will choose only one of two topics. For each topic there are three pictures. You will use the information from the question and the three pictures in your writing.

Story

See Test 1, Section 9, Option B on page 44.

Sample answer

Saying when the story happened.	Last summer Max had a fantastic time on a camping trip with his family. They stayed at a lovely place near
Describing the place.	a lake. His parents had a big tent to sleep in and Max had a smaller one. Max's mum built a fire and cooked
Saying what happened.	some sausages for lunch. Then they ate hot dogs and fruit. Max drank some lemonade and his father drank some tea. Later that day, they went to the lake. Max swam in the lake and his parents relaxed and watched Max swimming.

Exam help

- ✔ First, look carefully at both of the topics and all of the pictures before you decide which topic to choose. Think about which story you would find easier to tell and which one you know more vocabulary for.
- ✔ Make sure you know which type of text you need to write and how to organise your ideas.
- ✔ Decide whether you need to use *I* to write about something you did, (e.g. in a diary entry), or *he/she/they* or people's names to describe what other people did, e.g. in a description or a story.
- ✔ Check your grammar and make sure you use the right tenses in the right places in your story that will help you link your ideas together, e.g. *last summer; yesterday; while (I was walking); when (we went to the beach).* Make sure you use these correctly too.
- ✔ Make your story interesting by using lots of different vocabulary to describe the pictures or the events in the story. Also include how the people feel, what they are thinking or what they said.
- ✔ Try to use a variety of adjectives to add interest and excitement to your story (e.g. *fantastic, lovely*).
- ✔ Try not to repeat words. Think of words that mean the same (synonyms) instead of repeating the same word (for example, *nice → lovely → beautiful*).
- ✔ When you've finished writing, count the number of words in your text.

Useful language

Starting your story or description
Yesterday …
Last Saturday …
Last weekend …
Last summer …

Starting your diary entry
Saying where things happened
At the park/the beach/the cinema
At the entrance
At the concert
Near the lake/sea/beach
In the water

Saying when things happened
At first …
Then, …
After that …
After a while …
Later that day …
Finally, …

Saying why things happened
… decided to go to the park to listen to …
… because he didn't like dogs.
… it was raining so they went home.

Ending your text
They went home.
It was a great holiday.
They had a fantastic time.
Everyone felt happy/sad/excited/ very tired.

In a story
- You need verbs in the past tense (e.g. *stayed, had, cooked, built, ate*) because the story happened in the past.
- You need to use words that link the actions in the past (e.g. *Then, Later that day*) to make your story easy to follow.

Practice

1 **Look at Option A on page 44. What is the topic? Make a list of vocabulary words and phrases you can use to describe the three pictures. How many can you think of?**

2 **Complete the sentences with the adjectives or adverbs from the box. You can only use each word once.**

> badly   cheap   excited   interesting
> terrible

a The weather on the camping trip was
.... It rained all week.

b It was a very .... day.

c She hurt her leg .... when she feel out of the tree.

d Sarah was very .... to go to the concert. Her favourite band was playing.

e They are going shopping and the shop has a sign about .... shoes.

3 **Choose three pictures from a comic book, a cartoon or a story you see online. Then follow these steps:**

a Quickly make a list of the characters in your story or description, their names and any information about them.

b Plan the topic and the steps of the story or description.

c Make a list of the useful words and phrases you can use for the topic of the pictures.

d Write your story or description.

e Use the Checklist on this page to check your writing.

Planning your answer

Starting a story or a description

Start by taking some time to plan what you will write. Look carefully at both topics and choose the one you want to write about.

Make sure you know what kind of text you need to write (is it a story, a description or a diary entry?). Think about the kind of language you need to use for that kind of text.

Make a quick list of all the words and phrases you could use in a description or a story on that topic. Also think about the tenses you will need to use. Are you going to write about something that has happened in the past? How will you link your ideas for the story together? Who will be the characters in the story?

Writing your text

It is a good idea to write three paragraphs. Each paragraph can describe one of the three pictures.

How will you start your story in paragraph one? It is a good idea to think about a strong sentence that sets the scene first. Introduce the main character straight away and talk about where they are, what they are doing or how they feel. Then give more detailed information as they story goes on. Remember to link your ideas and sentences using linking words.

Something different is usually happening in the second picture. So this is a good place to make your story more interesting. Use a variety of vocabulary, phrases, adjectives and emotions to make it more interesting. Try to give as much information as you can.

The third paragraph describes the last picture. You want the reader to feel like the story is coming to an end. Use this paragraph to create a clear ending to your text. You can use speech, thoughts or feelings of the characters here to wrap the story up. Do you want the ending to be happy, sad or funny?

Finishing your story

When you have finished writing your text, you need to check it. Count the number of words, check your spelling and make sure that the story makes sense.

Checklist

When you finish writing your narrative, use this checklist.

Content

Does your story have a beginning and ending?

Have you used interesting vocabulary and structures?

Is your story clear?

Have you described all three pictures?

Communicative achievement

Is your style interesting?

Would you like to read this story yourself?

Language

Are your verb tenses correct?

Is your spelling and punctuation correct?

Does your email or letter make sense?

HOW TO PREPARE

Writing sections (Level 1, A2)

Sections 8 and 9 are the main Writing sections of the test. Section 8 tests your ability to write a piece of correspondence in response to input provided in the previous reading Section 7. Section 9 tests your ability to write a short narrative or descriptive text based on a series of pictures. It is important that you read the instructions for each section carefully and that the pieces of writing you produce are of the right length (neither too short nor too long). Here are some tips for dealing with each section of the Writing test:

Section 8: Writing correspondence

What happens in this section?

In Section 8 you will be asked to write a piece of correspondence: a short email, a letter, a postcard, a note or a blog entry in response to information provided in the Reading Section 7. You will be given a short text to read with clear instructions about the purpose of the piece of writing, who you are writing to and the content of the message. The word limit for this section is 50–70 words.

How can I prepare for this section?

Planning

Before you start any piece of writing, it is a good idea to plan what you are going to say. First, you need to think about who you are writing to and make sure you use the correct level of formality. The way you write to a friend, for example, is very different from the way you write to someone you've never met. Then, you need to think about why you are writing to them and make a list of all the points you need to cover. Make sure you cover all the points and avoid writing too much about one and not enough about others. It's a good idea to highlight the parts of the text in Reading Section 7 that you could use to help you plan the content of your piece of correspondence, but make sure you come up with some of your own ideas as well. Finally, you need to think about how you can begin and end your piece of correspondence and how you can link your ideas together to make it flow.

> **Who?**
> a friend
>
> **Why?**
> invite to your birthday party
>
> **What?**
> information about event
>
> **How?**
> what to say at the beginning/ in the middle/at the end.

> **Common mistakes**
>
> He go (goes) to school on (by) bus. People spend to (too) much time on social media.

Checking

Accurate spelling and grammar are important so make sure you leave a few minutes at the end of the task to check what you have written. You should read through your work once to look for spelling and punctuation errors and then read it again for grammar mistakes. It is a good idea to look back at past work you've done and make a list of errors you've made, particularly errors that you make again and again. If you're not sure why something is incorrect, ask your teacher to explain.

You also need to check that you haven't written too much or too little. The word limit for Section 8 is 50–70 words. You should try to keep within this range but don't worry if you are a few words under or over. You will only lose points if you write less than 40 words or more than 77 words.

Section 9: Story or descriptive text

What happens in this section?

The purpose of Writing Section 9 is to assess your ability to write a short narrative or descriptive text based on a series of pictures. The text can take the form of a diary entry, a short/photo story, a description or a recount. You will be given three pictures along with instructions regarding the intended audience and purpose of the text. The word limit for this piece of writing is 80–100 words.

How can I prepare for this section?

Planning

As for Section 8, it is important to plan what you are going to say before you start writing. First, read the instructions carefully and, as quickly as you can, decide which of the two alternative questions you are going to answer. To help you decide, you should think about how much vocabulary you know for each topic as it is important that you know enough words to write your answer.

When you've made your decision, go through the question carefully and highlight all the content points you need to cover. You can use these points to help you organise your answer into paragraphs. You should aim to write three paragraphs – one for each picture – but they don't all need to be the same length. The important thing is to make sure all the points are covered.

Finally, you need to think about how you can link your ideas together to make your writing flow. These kinds of linking words and phrases are important for all pieces of written work:

Language	Examples	Ideas for practicing
Time markers	Examples of these are *First, after that or a week ago*. They are very useful for storytelling and describing.	Make a list of time markers and add them to your vocabulary book.
Linking words	Words and phrases like *however, while, also, because* that are useful when you want to show you agree or disagree, or to give reasons and add more information.	Go back and look at something you have written. Can you use any of the words to link your ideas together, showing that you agree or disagree with something or to add more information?

Checking

As in Section 8, it's important to check your work to make sure you've completed the task as well as you can and that you haven't written too much or too little. The word limit for Section 9 is 80–100 words.

When you've finished, ask yourself these questions: *Have I covered all the points? Have I used interesting vocabulary? Have I used the correct tense? Are my points organised clearly?* It is also important to give yourself a few minutes to correct any obvious spelling, punctuation and grammar mistakes.

 *Go to the **Writing Bank** on pages 168–171 to find checklists to help you.*

ANSWER KEY

TEST 1

Test 1 Listening

Section 1 Training

Focus on the instructions

1 a ten; b three; c 10 seconds;
   d 10 seconds

Focus on the questions

1 the room number
2 where the bag is
3 In the conversation you'll probably hear all three clothes in the pictures. People change clothes because they're too big or too small, they don't like something or they don't need something.
4 a table
5 A A chef: food, kitchen, cook, oven
   B A nurse: hospital, doctor, patient, ill, sick
   C An office worker: computer, printer, desk, office, manager
6 Three buses. The first bus starts at 10 o'clock in the morning.
7 c
8 potatoes, eggs; fish
9 b
10 A: two girls; B: two girls and a boy; C: two girls and two boys

Focus on the language

1 a come; b above; c too; d table; e in; f leave; g out of; h got; i past; j three

Section 1 Test

1 C 'we're changing classrooms next week … please come to G34'
2 C 'I left my bag … On the shelf above the seat'
3 A 'the T-shirt … It's actually too short for me, so can I get a bigger size'
4 A 'a table by the window', 'I don't eat meat', 'several dishes without'
5 C 'The people in the office are really nice and I'm happy I don't work in the kitchen'

6 A 'Buses go from the bus station to Westside … starting from ten o'clock in the morning'
7 B 'Harrison's furniture factory … moving out of the city to a piece of land by the airport'
8 B 'it's got cream, fish and some vegetables in it'
9 B 'walk up Park Street … past some shops on your right. You'll see the hotel on the corner, before you turn into Winter Road'
10 B 'I'm going to play tennis tonight … Jane and I usually play against Steve and Harry, but Steve can't come. So there'll be just three of us'

Section 2 Training

Focus on the instructions

1 a You hear the recording twice.
   b You shouldn't write anything the first time you listen.
   c The second time you listen there are some pauses in the recording.
   d You must write what you hear.
   e You should check your spelling.

Focus on the questions

1 a When/What time
   b Which
   c When
   d off
2 film, phone, start, turn off, ticket. Students' own answers, e.g. seat, exit.
3 a, b, c, e

Focus on the language

1 The film will start in five minutes. Please find your seats now. If you have a phone, turn it off. We hope you enjoy the film.
3 The film will start in five minutes. // Please find your seats now. // If you have a phone, turn it off. // We hope you enjoy the film.
4 Hello and welcome to the show. There are some interesting people on the show today. We will talk about how to save money when you're shopping online. Then we

will talk about beautiful Norway and hear more about places to visit there too.

Section 2 Test

11 The film will start in five/5 minutes. Please find your seats now. If you have a phone, turn it off. We hope you enjoy the film.

Section 3 Training

Focus on the instructions

1 a five
   b an advertisement
   c a conversation (where a woman is asking for information)
   d two/twice

Focus on the questions

1 c
2 a language/the name of a language
3 a
4 reading, writing, listening, speaking, grammar, vocabulary
5 b
6 b
7 a number/a time
8 b, c or d
9 a

Focus on the language

1 a on, th
   b for
   c first
   d long
   e more
   f speaking

Section 3 Test

12 (the) 19th/19 'our next courses, which start on the 19th of September'
13 French 'and for the first time this year, we're giving French classes'
14 25/twenty-five 'Each course … is twenty-five weeks long'
15 speaking 'every lesson also includes a speaking exercise.'
16 BRISTOW/Bristow 'speak to Suzanne Bristow – that's B-R-I-S-T-O-W – at the school for more information'

17 Monday/Mon 'Next Monday, at nine thirty in the evening'

18 7:00/seven/7 (o'clock) 'Check-in starts at seven o'clock'

19 229761 'It's oh eight four three, double two nine, seven six one.'

20 train 'I'm coming on the train from my home'

21 15/fifteen '… it takes fifteen to walk'

Test 1 Reading

Section 4 Training

Focus on the instructions

1 a five
   b a cross
   c three
   d one

Focus on the questions

1 a 25 and 26
   b 22
   c 23 and 24
2 c
3 at a hotel (reception)
4 b
5 a
6 b
7 a check in
   c carry on

Focus on the language

1 b
2 knife
3 Because you can't/don't do the other things with a knife.
4 a
5 actors
6 Because you don't need actors for those two things.

Section 4 Test

22 A (We use 'cut' when we use a knife. We use 'mix' if we put things together, and 'wash' to clean something.)

23 B ('Party' is correct because it goes with 'groups of ten'. 'Bill' is about money, and 'service' is about the people who help customers in the restaurant.)

24 A ('Come back' is correct because it means returning at the end of the tour. 'Carry on' means to continue, and 'check in' means to go to a desk at a hotel to say that you have arrived.)

25 C ('Show' is correct because it goes with 'actors' and 'stars'. 'Band' is for people who play music or sing. A 'painting club' is for children to learn how to paint. An arts centre is a place where people go to watch bands and shows, not paint pictures.)

26 B ('Term' is correct because it means a period of time during the school year. There is a school holiday at the end of term. 'Library' is a place, not a time. 'Exam' is not correct because of school holiday.)

Section 5 Training

Focus on the instructions

1 a five
   b a cross
   c three
   d yes

Focus on the questions

1 a ii
   b A: a restaurant; B: a park; C: a cinema
   c all of them/three
   d The park: To describe where the restaurant is. The cinema: To say the restaurant isn't far from this place.
   e iii
   f iii
   g i
   h C is incorrect because the writer eats it **after** he does exercise (not before he does exercise).

Focus on the language

1 Classes start next week! Remember to get your college ID card from the Student Office this week. You'll need it to use the library during the course. Don't forget the welcome party next week; it'll be fun!

2 Remember to get your college ID card from the Student Office this week.
3 a & c
4 b
5 b
6 B

Section 5 Test

27 B ('It's important to eat before running … I usually have one or two bananas' Other people eat vegetables, not the writer. The writer eats chicken after exercising.)

28 B ('Classes start next week! Remember to get your college ID card … You'll need it to use the library')

29 B (B is correct because 'difficult to see' and 'you should stand closer' these show there is a problem with the photo. Pete likes the flower photo and the wedding photo.)

30 C (C is correct because it is for 'players under ten years old'. The cooking event is for 'adults only'. The music event is for 'over-18s'.)

31 A (A is correct because of 'please wear walking boots'. The text says 'don't bring any cash' so B is incorrect. 'You will be given lunch' means that students do not need to bring food with them, so C is also incorrect.')

Section 6 Training

Focus on the instructions

1 a an email
   b a magazine article
   c four
   d You write the answers.

Focus on the questions

1 a a day/a time
   b the name of a cinema
   c *Box 2* and *Dark House*
   d Tommy Jones' last film
2 a (the writer's) first camping trip
   b (the writer's) children
   c iii
   d (the writer's) new tent

Focus on the language

1 a i Friday. It's her brother's birthday party.
      ii Wednesday
   b 25 percent off
   c already
   d beautiful. It describes the music.
2 a (for) the first time
   b love
   c ii
   d six-person tent

Section 6 Test

32 (on) Wednesday: 'Shall we go on Wednesday?'
33 (the) Odeon: 'Let's go to the Odeon, not the Cineplex, because there's 25 percent off with your college card.'
34 Box 2: 'You've already seen Box 2.'
35 (the) music: 'the music was beautiful'
36 (with some) friends: 'I went camping for the first time … with some friends'
37 cooking food outside: 'The children love cooking food outside!'
38 (because of the) fresh air: 'I always sleep well on camping holidays. I think it's the fresh air!'
39 six/6: 'We've just bought a six-person tent'

Section 7 Training

Focus on the instructions

1 a an advertisement (for a competition)
   b notes
   c seven
   d no more than three

Focus on the questions

1 a
2 a
3 Canada (the other places are all cities in Canada)
4 a the last date to join the competition
   b the first date to perform in the competition
   c the last date to perform in the competition

5 when it will be on TV
6 cash prizes/money
7 c
8 c

Focus on the language

1 (young people who are) 13 to 18
2 c
3 no later than
4 b
5 pop, rock
6 fee

Section 7 Test

40 eighteen/18(years)(years old)
41 Canada
42 31 May/May 31/31.05/05.31/31st (of) May
43 (this)(in) September
44 cash prizes
45 (any) pop or rock (song)
46 $35/thirty-five dollars

Test 1 Writing

Section 8 Training

Focus on the instructions

1 a Section 7 (in the Reading section of the written test)
   b an email
   c Laura Duchamp (who is planning the competition)
   d 50–70 words

Focus on the questions

1 a You can sing on national television and you can win a cash prize.
   b Vancouver, Calgary, Toronto and Montreal
   c (her) email address
2 a three/3
   b i, iii & iv
   c iii, i, ii

Focus on the language

1 b
2 c
3 a
4 a
5 c
6 c
7 c

Section 8 Test

47 *Sample answer*
   Dear Laura,
   I'm excited about taking part in the New Stars singing competition. I want to enter the competition because I love singing and I want to be a famous singer one day!
   My aunt lives in Vancouver, so I'd prefer to sing in the competition you're having there. Is that possible? Do I need to bring anything with me, like a copy of my song?
   Regards,
   Belinda
   [68 words]

Section 9 Training

Focus on the instructions

1 a from three pictures (on the test paper)
   b 80–100

Focus on the questions

1 music or camping
2 a iii the two people in the pictures
   b ii a description
   c ii Going to see a band in the park.
3 a i a friend of yours
   b i went camping
   c i He enjoyed it.
4 Students' own answers. You should choose the topic that you find easiest and most interesting.

Focus on the language

1 c the past simple
2 at, to, but
3 a i last summer
   b ii Last summer Max had a great time on a camping trip with his family.
   c and
   d swam, relaxed, watched

Section 9 Test

48 A *Sample answer*
   Last Saturday, it was a really beautiful day. Monique and her friend Jess decided to go to the park

to listen to their favourite band. They met at the main entrance to the park and bought the tickets. At first the weather was very sunny and the music was great but after a while it started to get cloudy. Then it started raining very hard. The band stopped playing and Monique and Jess got really wet! They went home feeling sad.
[81 words]

B   *Sample answer*

Last summer, Max had a fantastic time on a camping trip with his family. They stayed at a lovely place near a lake. His parents had a big tent to sleep in and Max had a smaller one. Max's mum built a fire and cooked some sausages for lunch. Then they ate hot dogs and fruit. Max drank some lemonade and his father drank some tea. Later that day, they went to the lake. Max swam in the lake and his parents relaxed and watched Max swimming.
[87 words]

Test 1 Speaking

Section 10 Training

Focus on the instructions

1   a   1.5 minutes in total
    b   You speak on your own. The examiner starts by asking you a general question about yourself, and then asks another question about your experiences or your opinion about the topic from the first question. If there is still some time before the end of your one minute of speaking time, the examiner asks you one or more specific questions about the topic.
    c   Personal information questions, for example: food, travel, routines, hobbies, free time.

d   You speak for one minute. You don't need to spend one minute answering the first question. Say as much as you can, then the examiner asks another question. All of your answers are about one minute in total. The other 30 seconds are for the examiner to ask the questions.

Focus on the questions

1   What's your favourite food? Do you like cooking? What's your favourite way to travel? Do you enjoy travelling to new places? What is your favourite day of the week? Do you like getting up early? Do you enjoy going to museums?
2   b
3   c
4   a   Do you like cooking? Why/Why not?
    b   What did you eat yesterday?
    c   How often do you eat in restaurants or cafés? Who do you usually eat your meals with?
5   c
6   c (because it answers the question and gives a reason)
7   a & d
8   a   How are your weekends different from your weekdays?
    b   What did you do yesterday?
    c   What is your favourite day of the week? Do you like getting up early?

Focus on the language

1   c
2   What did you eat yesterday? How did you get here today? What did you do yesterday?
3   b
4   a because

Section 10 Test

Sample answers

TOPIC 1: FOOD

My favourite food is fruit.
I eat mostly fruit and vegetables, and sometimes fish.

Yes, I like cooking because it's fun and I can make what I want.
I don't eat in restaurants very often because it's expensive.
I had eggs for breakfast, and then I had pizza and salad when I went home yesterday.
I usually eat my meals with my parents.

TOPIC 2: TRAVEL

I travel to new places almost every year.
I love travelling by train.
I came here on the bus today.
I usually travel by bus, but sometimes I ride my bike.
I love going to new places because I can meet new people and see new things.
I usually read a book on a long journey.

TOPIC 3: HABITS and ROUTINES

I always get up at the same time every day, but I go to bed at different times.
I go to school and I do my homework every day.
My favourite day is Sunday, because I always meet with my family for breakfast and we spend a whole day together.
I went to the supermarket, and I also went swimming at the pool in town.
I like getting up early because the house is very quiet before other people get up.
I have more time to do sport at weekends. I can't do that in the week because I don't have time.

TOPIC 4: MUSEUMS

I love going to museums because I can see interesting things.
There's a big museum in my city – it has things from all over my country so it's very interesting.
I visit museums about three times each year.
I go to museums when I am on holiday.
I go with my family, or with my friends sometimes.
Yes, I think museums should be free, because then more people could go.

Section 12 Training

Focus on the instructions

1 a   a picture
   b   What you can see and what is happening in the picture.
   c   one minute
   d   Questions about details in the picture, e.g. What is he/she wearing?

Focus on the questions

1 a
2 b
3 a
4 a

Focus on the language

1 Students' own answers (for example: tourists, famous buildings, bus, city tour, take photos, guide, ride a bicycle)
2 Students' own answers (for example: city street, sports shop, sale, bus stop, friends talking, shopping)
3 b
4 a   (2)
   b   (1)
5 They are all listening to the guide, who is standing at the front.
6 She looks quite young, and she's wearing jeans and a shirt with flowers on it, and a hat. There's a man who's wearing a suit and tie, and carrying a briefcase.

Section 12A Test

Sample answer

I can see a city, with a tourist bus on the road. Three tourists are on the bus, two of them are sitting down and one is standing. There are two women who are about 20 or 30, and there's a man, he's a bit older, and he's got a cap on. They are all listening to the guide, who is standing at the front. He's wearing a cap too. One of the women is taking a photo of a big building. The guide is pointing to that building. It has steps outside, and there's a clock on the front of the building. The time is 1.30. On the road there is a woman who's riding a bike. She looks quite young, and she's wearing jeans and a shirt with flowers on it, and a hat. There's a man who's wearing a suit and tie, and carrying a briefcase. He's going to buy a newspaper.

Section 12B Test

Sample answer

I can see a street in a city, and I can see a shop window. The shop sells things like sports bags and footballs. There's a poster in the window, it says 'SALE' and '50% off'. Two boys are walking into the shop. One has glasses, and the other has a cap, and they're both wearing jeans. One has a T-shirt and the other one has a jacket. They are going to buy some things in the shop. Just next to the shop on the pavement is a bus stop and two women are sitting there. They're talking together. I think they're waiting for the bus, perhaps number D52 or G67, because those are the numbers on the bus stop. They are both wearing dresses, and one woman has got some shopping bags. They are smiling and laughing together.

Section 13 Training

Focus on the instructions

1 a   a (test-taker's) card
   b   (up to) 15 seconds
   c   you
   d   all of them
   e   about one minute

Focus on the questions

1 a   at the start of the task/role play
   b   at the end of the task/role play
   c   If the examiner gives you something or helps you.
   d   on your (test-taker's) card
   e   different questions in the role play
2 a, b & d

Focus on the language

1 b
2 a   How much, cost
   b   What does that ticket cost?

3 c
4 can
5 might
6 b

Section 13A Test

Sample answer

Hello,
Good morning. How can I help?
I'd like to buy a ticket for the boat please.
Of course. Do you want to go in the morning or the afternoon?
What time does the afternoon boat leave?
The boat leaves at 2.
How much is the ticket?
It's 10 euros per person.
OK, that's fine, thanks.
Here you are, thank you very much.
Goodbye.

Section 13B Test

Sample answer

Hello
Hello, can I help you?
Yes, I want to buy a book for my brother.
What sort of books does he like?
He loves books about travelling.
Well, I have a lovely book here that he might enjoy.
Thank you – how much is it?
It's £15.
I'll have it, thanks.
OK, thank you. Here you are.

TEST 2

Test 2 Listening

Section 1

1 C 'Maybe bananas … OK.'
2 B 'carry on along Castle Street. The park's on your left, opposite the library'
3 A 'we'll need long trousers'
4 C 'In our next lesson, we'll read the story'
5 C 'I'm going to a football match'
6 C 'The driver. She lives near us'

7 A 'Two tickets to see Lucy Brando, please – she's singing here'

8 C 'It will depart at 11:15'

9 B 'we'll give you a free pen'

10 A 'please eat your lunches in the staff room'

Section 2

11 Today, every school in the city was closed. This was because of last night's snow. Tomorrow, it will be much warmer. The schools will open again.

Section 3

12 8:30/half past eight/eight thirty 'We leave at half past eight'

13 museum 'go straight to the museum'

14 park 'it's time for lunch … we'll have it in the park.'

15 boat 'We're going to see London from a boat'

16 665401 'my phone number – it's 0788 665401'

17 LUBECK/Lubeck 'Can you spell that please? L-U-B-E-C-K.'

18 son 'It's my son – he's ill'

19 library 'I work in the library at the school'

20 (school) meeting 'I can't come to the meeting at school tonight'

21 Monday 'I'll be back at work after the weekend, on Monday'

Test 2 Reading

Section 4

22 A (A is correct because the heavy snow has made the train late. 'Arrive on time' is incorrect because the sign says, 'we are sorry about this'. C is incorrect because the train is coming 'from Manchester' so it can't 'leave soon')

23 B ('Join' is correct because it goes with 'us'. You 'take part' in something, and 'introduce us' is incorrect because the text is about starting an activity.)

24 A (A is correct because it goes with 'a problem' and it shows why the shop needs to be closed. B means the shop will create a problem, not stop the problem, so it is incorrect, and C is incorrect because you don't 'look for' a problem.)

25 C (C is correct because of 'the walls must be dry' and 'difficult to paint'. A and B are incorrect because 'warm' and 'light' walls are not 'difficult to paint'.)

26 B (B is correct because it is the only option which goes with 'to your seats'.)

Section 5

27 C (Options A and B are incorrect because hats and coats are not included in the summer sale. They are coming in the autumn.)

28 C ('I can't wait to get to my new flat next week! The first thing I'll do is clean it.' A is incorrect because Julia doesn't say she will first hang the picture in the bedroom. B is incorrect because Julia has 'already packed' her boxes.)

29 B ('…our lovely new chocolate cake'. Option A is not correct because it is 'famous' but it doesn't say that it has changed. Option C is not correct because the restaurant has always cooked chicken and rice the same way 'cooked the same great way for over fifty years.')

30 A (Option B is incorrect because 'the music club is already full', and option C is incorrect because it is only for 'girls to join the Year 9 team')

31 B ('Erdley School has a free school bus which most pupils use.')

Section 6

32 fourteen/14 (years old): 'It's her first international competition next month, just after her fourteenth birthday.'

33 (to) learn new skills/because she's excited about learning new skills: 'she's excited about taking part to learn new skills'

34 (in the) south: 'Darcy's home town is in the south'

35 (a local) gym: 'A local gym is paying for her travel costs'

36 two (university) students: 'I share a flat with two university students.'

37 because it's in the city centre: 'It's perfect because it's in the city centre.'

38 (by) train: 'I take the train to get to my lessons.'

39 meeting other people: 'the best thing is meeting other people'

Section 7

40 14(th) November/November 14(th)/14.11/11.14

41 coach

42 9:15(am/a.m.)/nine fifteen/quarter past nine

43 (the) 1960s/60s/(the)(nineteen) sixties

44 (the)(first) mobile phones/mobiles

45 computer game

46 (a)(your)(your own) lunch

Test 2 Writing

Section 8

47 *Sample answer* (*email*)

Hi Jessie,
Next week, my class is going to the Computer Museum. When I'm there, I'm going to see the computer games my mum and dad played as kids.
I love class trips because I think they are a good way to learn new information and it's nice to be out of the classroom too.
Do you like going on class trips?
Best wishes,
Thomas
[65 words]

Section 9

48 A *Sample answer*

Last weekend, I met my friend Carlos in a coffee shop in town. It was raining so we decided to go to the cinema. There was a new

film on which looked good, so we decided to see that. We bought our tickets, found our seats and waited for the film to start. It was very long – over 2 hours – but we enjoyed it. The actors were great and the story was very interesting. I'd like to see it again one day.
[82 words]

B   Sample answer

On Tuesday, a journalist came to my school to talk about her job. She writes for a successful travel magazine. Her last job was in China. She travelled there to visit lots of places that tourists love to visit, like the Great Wall of China. She always writes notes about the places she visits. She wrote about the trip to China on the plane home. Her story was in last month's magazine and she saw it when she went into a bookstore in her town. She felt very pleased.
[89 words]

Test 2 Speaking

Section 10
Sample answers

TOPIC 1: MUSIC
I listen to music every day.
People my age listen to pop music.
I listen to music when I'm on the bus, or when I'm at home.
My sister can play the guitar.
Yes, I went to a concert in my town last year.
Yes, I do. I buy music on the internet a lot.

TOPIC 2: HOBBIES
I don't have much free time.
I like swimming and playing computer games.
I want to learn to paint pictures, because I enjoy playing with different paints and brushes.
My dad likes reading and my mum likes cycling.

I like playing computer games because I can play with my friends and it's exciting.
Yes, it's easy, because there are lots of different games to choose from.

TOPIC 3: PLACE WHERE YOU LIVE
I live in a city.
I live in the middle of the city in a large apartment.
I like the main shopping street near my apartment.
There are lots of clothes shops and a big supermarket.
There is a cinema and a sports centre for young people.
There are two big parks that tourists like visiting.

TOPIC 4: CLOTHES
I like wearing sports clothes.
I like wearing blue or black clothes best.
Yes, I wear the same things because at my school we can wear what we want.
I usually buy my clothes online.
I don't like shopping for clothes because it takes too long.
I only keep my clothes for a few months because I like to have new things.
Then, I give the old clothes to my friends and family.

Section 12A
Sample answer

I can see a park, and it is a sunny day. There are some teenagers in the park and they are playing football. There are six of them, three boys and three girls. Four of them are wearing jeans and T-shirts, and there are two boys who are wearing shorts. One girl is smiling – she scored a goal. There is a small lake in the park and there are three birds swimming on it. Near the lake there's a woman and a young girl, perhaps her daughter. The little girl is looking at the birds. The woman's wearing a skirt and she is showing the birds to her daughter. Her daughter's wearing a skirt too. Theirs is also a café, and there's a sign outside which says 'Coffee 1 euro'.

Section 12B
Sample answer

I can see a living room, with some people in it. There's a man who is on the sofa. He's watching a programme on a big TV. Perhaps it is a film. In the film there's someone riding a horse. The man is holding a cup and there is a plate of biscuits on a small table in front of him. There's a bigger table in the room, and there's a boy who looks about 13, and he's playing with a computer tablet. He's laughing. There is a woman who is sitting in an armchair. She is reading a newspaper. She's wearing glasses, trousers and a jumper. She's got her phone on the chair near her. There's a clock on the wall and the time is 8.30.

Section 13A
Sample answer

Hello, I want some information about tennis classes, please.
Yes of course. There is a class in the morning or in the afternoon. Which would you like?
What time does the afternoon class start?
The class is at 3 p.m.
How long is the class?
An hour and a half. It finishes at 4:30
When do I pay for the class?
You can pay when you come to the class.
Thank you.
You're welcome.

Section 13B
Sample answer

Hello!
Hello – how can I help you?
Are there any tickets for the film at 6 o'clock, please?
Yes, there are plenty. How many would you like?
I would like four tickets please.
OK. And do you want any snacks too?
What do you have?
We've got chocolates, ice creams and drinks.
I would like ice cream, please.
OK, here you are. Thanks.
Thanks.

TEST 3

Test 3 Listening

Section 1

1   C 'Mr Matthews is starting a tennis club.'
2   B 'I've got to do a project on how mountains are made now – I need one on that.'
3   B 'What's it about? The history of medicine.'
4   A 'This week only, we have a half-price sofa sale.'
5   A 'we're too close to the screen … I like the actors'
6   B 'bedrooms … we wanted two and it's only got one … the kitchen's next to the living room'
7   A 'my week on a boat was actually a lot of fun'
8   A 'we've got a new chicken dish which is fantastic'
9   B 'now we're learning how plants grow'
10 C 'We have a video call every week.'

Section 2

11 The science museum/The Science Museum is in the city centre. It is in a very large, old building. You can learn a lot about the world there.

Section 3

12 White 'we're going to pick up rubbish from White Sands beach'
13 bus 'I've hired a bus for everyone.'
14 £2.50/two pounds fifty 'for students, £2.50 return'
15 plastic 'there's lots of rubbish. Most of it is plastic'
16 party 'Then, after all our hard work, we'll have a party.'
17 (the) 21st/twenty-first 'no, sorry, the 21st of June. It's a Saturday.'
18 Thexton 'It's 10, Thexton Road. That's spelt T-H-E-X-T-O-N.'
19 second/2nd 'And what floor's the flat on? The second floor'
20 supermarket 'go to the supermarket – the car park there is free'
21 picture 'And I'd like to buy something for the flat … a picture?'

Test 3 Reading

Section 4

22 A (A is correct because of 'try different lessons and … help you choose the right course'. Students don't generally choose a classroom. 'School' is incorrect because the Open Day is for students at the school: 'our students.')
23 B (B is correct because it explains why people should 'use the toilets on the second floor', so 'ready' is incorrect. 'Open' is incorrect because the sign says people should 'use the toilets on the second floor instead', so they cannot use the first-floor toilets.)
24 B (B is correct because the job requires 'own vehicle' and is for 'Bobby's Taxis'. A is not correct because it doesn't go with taxi. C is used for planes, not taxis.)
25 C (A is incorrect because it doesn't go with 'choose our coffee' and the customer 'drinks' the coffee, not the company. B is incorrect because the coffee company visits the farms; it doesn't make the coffee. C is correct because it goes with 'choose our coffee'.)
26 A (A is correct because it goes with 'on the screen'. B and C are incorrect because they don't mean buying a ticket by touching the screen.)

Section 5

27 C (Option A is incorrect because 'the engineer is coming to fix the problem with the internet', option B is incorrect because 'I'll be back from the supermarket' meaning Andy. C is the correct answer 'you can get the flat ready for the party'.)
28 B ('Holly's pictures of birds won.' Options A and C are incorrect because cash and new computers were prizes in the competition.)
29 C (Option A is incorrect because it describes Great Ripton – bridge, café and river. Option B is incorrect as this is the garden at Longton Hall. Option C is correct 'Great Heston, where you'll find the Moors Art Centre'.)
30 B ('You might not see the female elephants …' Options A and C are incorrect because you will still be able to see them. The lions may get angry and the monkeys 'may steal your lunch'.)
31 A ('… the Royal Theatre tonight. Let's try that!'. Option B is incorrect because Jenny is 'going to the gym soon' and option C is incorrect as 'I don't want to go dancing'.)

Section 6

32 meeting Leon Jackson: 'the best part was meeting Leon Jackson'
33 clothes: 'I'd love to do the same but with clothes.'
34 (how to) build a website: 'He … showed me how to build a website …'
35 make (my/some/his/her own) business cards: 'I've decided to start making my business cards.'
36 (for) twenty years: 'Over her twenty-year cooking career…'
37 French (food/cooking): 'everyone knows Rhea's TV shows about French cooking'
38 her father: 'Her father … taught her to cook. "My love of food comes from him"'
39 (the) loud music: 'not everyone loves the loud music'

Section 7

40 Fridays/Friday
41 (the) (school) library
42 noon/12(pm/p.m.)/twelve (o'clock)
43 Island Boy
44 3/three weeks
45 free/nothing
46 snacks

Section 8

47 Sample answer (email)

Hi Sam,

Have you heard about the new book club called Read Up? Everyone meets in the school library on Fridays and discusses a book. They choose what to read three weeks before and there are snacks, too!

I really want to join because I love reading and it's a great way to meet new people.

Do you want to come with me? Let me know soon!

Faith

[68 words]

Section 9

48 A Sample answer

My friend Mark enjoys cooking new things. He is very good at baking cakes and last Friday, he decided to make a chocolate cake. He had everything he needed at home, so he mixed eggs, flour, sugar and milk together, and some chocolate, of course. Then he put the cake in the oven. It took about an hour to cook. Mark texted me and two of our friends and invited us to come to his house. When we arrived, we ate Mark's cake and it was delicious!

[87 words]

B Sample answer

Last Friday, I went out for dinner with my college friends. We met at the college and talked about what to eat and where to go. We decided to try the new burger restaurant called V-Rev. I'm glad we booked a table immediately because it was very busy. It looked really cool inside – like an old American restaurant from the 1950s. The menu had lots of different burgers. I ordered the 'classic' with fries and a milkshake. We didn't have to wait long for our food and we had a great time!

[92 words]

Section 10

Sample answers

TOPIC 1: ROUTINES

I like weekends best.

I usually go shopping with my family.

Sometimes yes, because it's fun to do new things.

Last weekend, I went to buy some shoes.

I am very busy in the week because I have lots of homework to do.

No, I don't work at the weekend. I prefer to spend my weekends playing tennis or swimming with my friends.

TOPIC 2: WEATHER

It's hot and sunny.

In summer, it's hot, but in winter, it rains a lot.

I like it when it's not too hot.

I prefer very hot weather, because I can go to the beach.

I don't like when it's raining.

When it's hot I wear shorts and when it rains I wear a coat.

TOPIC 3: ACCOMMODATION

I live in an apartment.

It's quite big and has five rooms.

My parents and my sister live with me.

My favourite place is the kitchen, because we all like to sit and talk in there.

Yes, it's the right size because everyone has a bedroom and the living room is large.

I'd like to buy a new poster for my room.

TOPIC 4: FILMS

Not really, because I like lots of films.

I like watching comedies and thrillers.

I usually watch films with my friends.

I prefer to go to the cinema.

My favourite actor is Leonardo DiCaprio. I think he's very good at acting.

I love watching films from other countries because I can learn a lot about different cultures.

Section 12A

Sample answer

In the picture, there is a large room, with some tables. Five people are sitting at one of the tables. They are eating sandwiches and drinking something. There are two women, and they are wearing dresses, and one has a scarf. There's a handbag on the floor. There are three men too, and they're wearing trousers and shirts. Only one of them is wearing a tie. Two of them are wearing glasses, and everyone is laughing. There's a woman in the background who is serving something – she's holding a plate of cupcakes and there's a teapot in front of her. There's a big clock on the wall, and the time is 3:15.

Section 12B

Sample answer

I can see a street with some people and a bus. It's a sunny day. There's a man who looks quite young, he's sitting on a bench looking at another man who is coming down the road. The man who is sitting is wearing a jacket and jeans and he has a phone. The other man seems very stylish. He's also got a phone. He's smiling and waving, and he's wearing sunglasses and jeans and a shirt. There's a bus coming, it's number 31. There are two small girls with their dad, they're wearing shorts and T-shirts, and they're holding hands and laughing.

Section 13A

Sample answer

Hello, can you help me with my party?

Yes, of course – shall I bring some food?

Can you bring some fruit, please?

OK. When is the party?

It's on Saturday.

OK – I'll see you there.

Can you come early to help me?

Yes, of course – what time?

Can you come at 6, please?

Sure! You're welcome!

Section 13B

Sample answer

Hello, it's George, I'm sorry I'm late!

That's OK – what happened?
I missed the bus!
Oh dear! When will you get here?
I'll arrive in about 20 minutes.
OK, I'll wait till you get here to order anything.
OK, bye.
Bye!

TEST 4

Test 4 Listening

Section 1

1 B 'We only have time to go to the market'
2 B 'Now, it's the football match'
3 A 'we must always put plastic gloves on'
4 C 'You play the guitar really well … I'm practising some music that my students are learning. Is that the only instrument you teach? Yes'
5 B 'He's actually quite young, with curly dark hair.
6 C 'When I try to open or lock the car door with it, or try to start the engine, nothing happens'
7 B 'I thought the painting with lots of squares was brilliant … I agree – certainly the best one'
8 A 'I'd prefer to be an aeroplane engineer.'
9 B 'you're in room fifteen. That's on the first floor.'
10 A 'the lake there is full of rubbish. We're going to clean it up.'

Section 2

11 A new restaurant has just opened in town. You can get all kinds of dishes there. Everything is quite cheap. It's already very busy.

Section 3

12 school 'it's by the school'
13 25/twenty-five 'cheaper for you then – only twenty-five pounds'
14 classes 'And that includes … ? Gym equipment … but not classes.'
15 10/ten p.m. 'Seven a.m. until ten p.m. Sunday to Friday'

16 shop 'does King Street gym have a café? No, just a shop.'
17 Tuesday 'It's an evening course, and lessons are on a Tuesday.'
18 North 'Lessons are in the art room, which is in the North Building'
19 (the) 16th/sixteenth 'our first lesson's on the 16th'
20 people 'You'll learn to paint various subjects, starting with people.'
21 entrance 'we'll have a show of your paintings. We'll put this in the entrance to the college'

Test 4 Reading

Section 4

22 B (B is correct because it means the visitors will not have them in the hall. 'Leave' goes with 'at reception'. Option A is incorrect because we need to say give something 'to' reception. Option C is incorrect because we have to say 'receive them from reception'.)
23 A (A is correct because it goes with 'lights and lock' and it is the only option which goes with the 'seat moves up and down'. Bike seats need to move up and down because people are different heights.)
24 A (A is correct because it goes with 'road … is closed … if you are driving'. B is incorrect because it doesn't go with 'driving' – it means travelling by bus or train. C is incorrect because the problem is with the road, not the vehicle.).
25 C (C is correct because it goes with 'small cats … large cats'. A and B are incorrect because 'small … large' do not relate to shape or age.
26 A (A is correct because it goes with 'run near the swimming area', and it goes with 'happen'. B and C do not go with 'run near the swimming area' they happen in water.)

Section 5

27 C (People 'get 10 percent off all chocolate at the factory shop'

means that people have to pay for the chocolate. Option C is correct because it says 'a free drink' and option A says 'you can buy local food like … cake' which means you pay for it as well.)
28 C ('The key's behind the bin by the window'. A is incorrect because of 'I've moved the house key. It was under the plant pot by the front door but …', B is incorrect because it talks about the garage key, not the house key. '… the garage key, it's on the kitchen table.')
29 A ('Many people find drinking milk helps them sleep when it's very hot.' B and C are incorrect because they are not about sleeping.)
30 B ('Parents enjoy helping them' means that both parents and children do the activity together. Options A and C are for children to do alone.)
31 C ('We also need students to help clean the local park'. Option A is for students who are 'studying to become a teacher', and option B is for students who can drive.)

Section 6

32 buy (her) coursebooks: 'Before the term begins, please buy your coursebooks. You'll need them on the first day of class.'
33 Jan Williams: 'Jan Williams will be the person to contact for any problems with your classes.'
34 £5,000 (a year): 'college bedrooms … cost £5,000 a year.'
35 (in) private accommodation: 'Second-year students have to rent private accommodation'
36 (a) small (football club): 'It's about players at a small football club'
37 (that) it isn't easy to work (there/ in the football industry): 'the programme … , it also shows that it isn't easy to work in the football industry.'
38 (because) it doesn't show female players: 'People watching the show

and women's sports organisations are sad that Football Dreams doesn't show female players.'

39 female runners: 'the TV company is making a programme about female runners'

Section 7

40 Belgium
41 car
42 hotel
43 9:30(am)/half past nine/half nine/ nine thirty
44 53/fifty-three
45 (very) hot
46 T-shirt

Test 4 Writing

Section 8

47 *Sample answer* (email)

I'd like to join the Top Speed cycling club so I can meet people my age who like cycling as much as I do. I got my first bike when I was only 5 and now, I'm 14. I can cycle quite fast but I've never been in a competition before.
Could you please give me some more information about the club? How often do you meet?
Thanks,
Jamie
[69 words]

Section 9

48 A *Sample answer*

On Saturday, it was a beautiful sunny day so my friend and I decided to have a picnic at the park. We found a place to sit under a big tree. We put a blanket on the ground and took out some sandwiches, a bar of chocolate and some juice from our shopping bag. When we were eating the bar of chocolate, a bird flew down from the tree and took one of our sandwiches. We were very surprised and we thought it was funny that the bird ate some of our picnic!
[93 words]

B *Sample answer*

My friend Lisa is a really good artist. She can draw people and animals very well. For her grandfather's birthday, she wanted to draw him a special picture. She decided to draw a picture of her grandfather sitting on a chair with his pet cat. She used a photo to help her with the drawing. It took her a week – she did it every day after school. Lisa gave her grandfather the drawing at his birthday party. When he saw the picture, he was very happy – and so was his cat!
[91 words]

Test 4 Speaking

Section 10

Sample answers
TOPIC 1: WORK

I'd love to be a doctor.
I think jobs that make you happy and let you help other people are good jobs.
My mother is a nurse and my father is a teacher.
Yes, I think it's better to work near where you live.
I wouldn't want to be a police officer as it's sometimes dangerous.
Yes, but only if you like travelling and seeing different places.

TOPIC 2: READING

Yes, I enjoy reading very much.
It's a book about a famous football player I read last month.
We don't really, because we all like reading different things.
I didn't read very much when I was younger. I preferred watching videos.
My favourite writer is called Laura Stillers because she writes exciting books.
I prefer reading books because I think it's relaxing.

TOPIC 3: HOLIDAYS

Of course, I love going on holiday!
I went to the mountains for a week.

I go on holiday once a year.
Yes, I usually go on holiday in my country. It has lots of interesting places to see.
It's best to go in the summer when the weather is good.
I like going to the beach most because there is lots to do there, for example, you can go for a swim or play beach volleyball. So I think the seaside is the best place to spend a holiday.

TOPIC 4: ANIMALS

Yes, I like animals.
My favourite animal is a cat.
Yes, there are lots of programmes about animals and they're very popular in my country.
You can see cows and sheep, and other animals like goats.
No, I don't have a pet at the moment.
I think hamsters are good pets because they are easy to look after and very beautiful.

Section 12A

Sample answer

I can see a big room with a few chairs in it and a sofa. There are two women sitting there, drinking coffee. They're wearing jeans and sweatshirts. There's a radio on a table near them with music playing, and a lamp and a computer. There's a TV on the wall and on the screen, I can see a boat on the sea. A young man is standing in the room, and he's reading something on a notice board. He's wearing sports clothes and he's got a tennis racket. There's a poster saying 'Student Party'. There's a bookcase in the room with some magazines and some books on it. There's a plant on top of the bookcase, as well as a coffee cup.

Section 12B

Sample answer

I can see two fields in the picture. It looks like the countryside. To the left of one of the fields there is a train line with a train going past. There's a big tree in the middle of that field. There are three cows in the other field. There's a family in the field in front of the tree, and they're having a picnic on a blanket. The mother is wearing a dress and the dad is wearing shorts and a shirt. There are two young girls with their parents. They're wearing T-shirts and skirts. The people are eating sandwiches and apples. Their car is parked at the side of the road by a gap in the hedge. There are two planes in the sky.

Section 13A

Sample answer

Hi!

Hi, do you know what time Sam's party starts this weekend?

Yes, it starts at 7.30.

Thanks. What are you taking for a present? I'm not sure what to get …

I'm taking a book because he loves reading.

Good idea! How are you getting there?

I'm driving – do you want to come with me?

It's OK thanks, I'm going with my brother, so I'll see you there! Bye!

Bye!

Section 13B

Sample answer

Hello, when does the next train to the city leave please?

It goes in 30 minutes.

Which platform does it go from?

It leaves from platform number 7.

And where can I buy tickets?

There's a ticket office just behind you.

Oh thanks! What time does the station café close?

It closes at 6 p.m.

Thanks.

You're welcome.

Test 5 Listening

Section 1

1 B 'put your bags under your seats'
2 B 'tomorrow will bring a big change, as rain arrives from the west'
3 A 'The topic's "Machines"'
4 C 'Does she make the clothes? No, she gets them from a local factory and sells them in her online store.'
5 B 'between the bookshop and the lifts'
6 A 'The only thing we can't do is eat in class.'
7 A 'They've increased the size of their seats'
8 B 'Actually, along the road.'
9 A 'I couldn't believe how good it was'
10 C 'please remember to wash your kit before then'

Section 2

11 Take your new printer out of the box. To start using it, first turn on the power. Then put paper in it. Now it is ready to use.

Section 3

12 trees 'there are plenty of trees'
13 15/fifteen 'The walk takes fifteen.'
14 west 'Are there any cafés at the beach? There are two at the west end.'
15 Fish 'but you can go to Fish Island'
16 543922 'It's 0768 543922.'
17 children 'On Wednesday evenings, I have a class just for children'
18 advanced 'on Thursday evenings I teach classes for advanced singers'
19 90 'But I'm offering ten lessons for £90 if you book before the 30th of September'
20 concert 'You can find me online, and see some of my students singing in a concert.'
21 TOPSET 'email me at Maria@T-O-P-S-E-T.com'

Test 5 Reading

Section 4

22 C (C is correct because it goes with 'end-of-season', 'finish soon' and 'ending 14 Jan'. Options A and B do not go with time but are the items people can buy.)
23 A (A is correct because birds have wings but mice and dogs don't.)
24 A (A is correct because it goes with 'locked' and 'let into the building'. 'Garage' and 'cupboard' can be locked but they don't go with 'ring the bell to be let into the building.')
25 B (B is correct because it goes with 'show on a big …' and 'films'. A is incorrect because you cannot show something on a theatre. C is incorrect because it doesn't go with 'show on a big'.)
26 A (A is correct because we can 'pass through' a gate to show a movement. B and C do not go with 'gate'.)

Section 5

27 B ('No swimming in the river.' Not A as cameras are allowed in the park 'Our guides will show you where to take the best photos' and not C as eating is allowed 'put … after eating')
28 C ('The industry which interested the highest number of students was computer technology, where most students wanted to be engineers.' A and B are students' reasons why they chose business or teaching.)
29 A ('The business wasn't doing very well because more people buy clothes online now.' Option B is not correct that business closed 'two months ago', and option C is a new business.)
30 A ('when you just need to forget your stress and relax, there's nothing better than a long walk outside.' Option B 'can make us even more tired', Option C 'can give us more energy', which is not the same as relaxation.)

31 B ('My school doesn't use plastic bottles'.)

Section 6

32 art: 'Fenstowe … it is the area's capital of art.'

33 a shoe factory: '… Phillips Centre. This was once a shoe factory.'

34 photos: 'There's 10 percent off all photos for our tour group.'

35 wood: '… Bob Danson, an artist who makes beautiful things out of wood.'

36 (human) biology: 'her work on human biology'

37 ten/10 (books): 'All her ten books have been translated'

38 science students: 'Science students must be at this event'

39 continue their education: 'Dr Woolton's organisation which helps science students … to continue their education.'

Section 7

40 Market Square

41 (for) (one/a) (whole) week

42 (by) bus

43 (some) (fish) soup

44 (French) cheese

45 pasta

46 (a) cookbook

Test 5 Writing

Section 8

47 *Sample answer* (email)

Hi Lily,

As you know, I'm from the UK and my favourite dish is fish and chips. I believe almost every town in the UK has a fish and chip shop as many people enjoy eating it. They usually have it when they go out, but I don't think it's healthy!

I really like reading food blogs because I can learn about healthier options.

Best,

James

[66 words]

Section 9

48 A *Sample answer*

One time my friend Jessica invited me to go for a boat ride with her. Our town is near a big lake so Jessica's parents have a boat. It was a really hot day, so I was happy to do something fun and relaxing. We spent some time driving a boat and then lying on the grass and enjoying the sun. My friend even read a book. It was a great day and I think Jessica had a lot of fun too!

[82 words]

B *Sample answer*

Last winter, I had a fantastic day that I'll never forget. One morning, while I was having breakfast with my family, we heard some interesting news on TV. The weather presenter said that all the schools were closed because of heavy snow! I immediately called my best friend to tell her and we decided to meet in the park. When we arrived there, the park looked beautiful with snow everywhere. We saw lots of friends from school playing in the snow and a few people were even having a big snowball fight!

[92 words]

Test 5 Speaking

Section 10

Sample answers

TOPIC 1: FRIENDS

I usually spend time with friends at weekends.

Most of my friends live near me, and we work together too.

I like going to restaurants with my friends.

Friends can go anywhere together, like shopping centres or even on holiday. We use our phones to contact each other.

I have a best friend who I met at school. We spend a lot of time together because we play in a band!

TOPIC 2: COMPUTERS

I use a computer every day.

I use it for work, and also for getting information about the news and things like that.

Probably about five, I was very young!

Yes, the internet is very useful because you can find things you need quickly.

I don't have one favourite website, but I generally like sports websites.

I take my laptop with me on holiday so I can watch films.

TOPIC 3: SPENDING TIME OUTSIDE

I spend a lot of time outside.

I like walking and going to the park.

People can go for walks along the river or in the park.

I often go outside with my friends or my family.

Last time, I went to a river near my house with my friends and we had a picnic.

Yes, I would because it's a good way to keep fit and you can see different things.

TOPIC 4: TELEVISION

Yes, I like watching TV.

I watch TV almost every day.

My favourite programme is one about a family, it's called *The Dawsons*.

I watch TV in the living room.

Yes, my sister and I like to watch together so we can talk about what's happening.

I don't like advertisements because there are too many on TV now.

Section 12A

Sample answer

I can see four young women, and they're standing talking together. They're in a hotel. There is a reception desk at the back of the picture, with a receptionist who is wearing a uniform, and he's talking on the phone. Two of the women are wearing dresses, one is wearing a skirt and a shirt, and one is wearing trousers and a jacket. One woman has a hat on, and two are wearing glasses. On the walls there are three big paintings. I can see a big building, like a castle, in one, and the other two look very modern. There is a coat and umbrella hanging up in the reception, and a large mirror on the wall.

Section 12B
Sample answer

I can see a beach. There are two young boys in the water, throwing a ball to each other. There are two young girls eating ice creams. They are wearing skirts, T-shirts and hats. There is a woman taking a photo of them and they are smiling. There is a small shop on the beach that sells things like water and ice creams and a man is buying a bottle of water. There are two teenagers, one girl who is wearing jeans and a shirt and a teenage boy who's wearing jeans and T-shirt standing, waiting to buy something. The sun is shining, and there is a big ship further out in the sea.

Section 13A
Sample answer

Hello, I want to do an art class, please.
Hello, we have classes every day at 5 – which would you like?
I want to come on Thursdays please.
That's fine, we have places then.
When do I pay for the class?
You can pay on the first day.
What do I need to bring?
Just bring a snack – we provide everything else.
Thank you. Goodbye.
Goodbye.

Section 13B
Sample answer

Hello, I want to get a bus to the beach, please.
Of course. We have buses all day.
I want to go at 11.
OK, there's one just after that.
Where does it leave from?
You need to go to stop 4, at the bus station entrance.
What time is the last bus back?
The last one is at 7:45 – don't miss it!
Thanks, goodbye.
You're welcome – goodbye.

GRAMMAR BANK

There *is*/*are*

1. a there is
   b there are
   c there isn't
   d there are
2. a There is
   b There are
   c There are
   d There is
3. a 's/is
   b 's/is
   c are
   d are
   e 's/is
   f are
   g 's/is
   h are

Countable and uncountable nouns: *some* and *any*

1. a U
   b C
   c U
   d U
   e C
   f C
   g U
   h C
2. a some
   b some
   c any
   d any
   e some
3. a any
   b some
   c any
   d some
   e any
   f any

The definite article: *the*

1. a I love **the** Brazilian people we met yesterday.
   b Who is **the** boy you sit next to in class?
   c Dad, I need to use **the** car.

d **The** Moon is very bright tonight.
e When is **the** test?

Prepositions

1. a at
   b in
   c in
   d on
   e up
   f down

Present simple

1. a do (you) do
   b like
   c Does (your sister) play
   d doesn't/does not like
   e does (your sister) do
   f bakes
2. a spends
   b go
   c goes
   d doesn't/does not (usually) buy
   e listen
   f like
   g don't sound/do not sound

Adverbs of frequency

1. a doesn't often go
   b never
   c sometimes
   d usually
2. a We never watch films in the morning.
   b They aren't usually late.
   c My mum often sings in the car.
   d Basketball club is always on a Friday.
   e Daria doesn't often go shopping.

Much/*many*

1. a many
   b much
   c many
   d much
   e many

Present continuous

1. a 'm not
   b is
   c am
   d isn't
   e are
2. a 're/are learning
   b isn't/is not listening
   c is showing
   d 're/are building
   e 'm/am not feeling
3. a Are you enjoying your computer club
   b We're/are learning so many new things
   c are you doing at the moment
   d is showing us how to make a vlog
   e I'm/I am making a vlog about animals
   f is doing a sports vlog

Present simple and present continuous

1. a 'm writing
   b get
   c click
   d 'm watching
   e 'm taking
   f I usually check
2. a do (you) send
   b Is (your phone) ringing
   c do (you) visit
   d Is (Harry) playing
   e do (you often) use
3. a Are (you) having
   b 'm/am enjoying
   c is
   d 's/is raining
   e 're/are staying
   f 're/are visiting
   g 'm/am standing

Present simple questions: how

1. a How
   b How big
   c How often
   d How long
   e How much
   f How many

Past simple

to be

1. a was
   b were
   c wasn't
   d weren't
   e was
   f Were

Regular verbs
Irregular verbs
Time expressions with the past simple

1. a were
   b read
   c talked
   d took
   e won
2. a travelled
   b started; finished
   c didn't/did not study; didn't/did not feel
   d ran; were
   e gave

Past simple questions and short answers

1. a Did you like your primary school?
   b Where were you two hours ago?
   c Did you finish the last exercise?
   d Did you arrive late this morning?
2. a Where
   b Did
   c Were
   d Was

Comparative and superlative adjectives

Comparative adjectives

1. a larger
   b sunnier
   c more beautiful
   d fatter
   e longer
   f more difficult
   g wetter
2. a quieter
   b prettier
   c older; taller
   d more crowded
   e lighter
3. a more fun than
   b easier
   c bigger
   d more interesting than

Superlative adjectives

1. a the noisiest
   b the worst
   c the strangest
   d the most careful
   e the shortest
   f the most popular
   g the happiest
2. a the lowest
   b the quietest
   c the most comfortable
   d the sunniest
   e the fattest

Past continuous

1. a was
   b were
   c wasn't
   d was
   e weren't
2. a were (you) doing
   b was playing
   c were having
   d were watching
   e wasn't working
   f were complaining
   g weren't watching

Be going to

1. a We're going to ride around the lake.
   b Elisa is going to fly a helicopter.
   c You aren't going to get the train.
   d They are going to sleep on the ship.
   e Is Jack going to wait on the platform?
2. a going to buy; he is
   b going to travel; they aren't
   c going to arrive; we are
   d going to get; she isn't
   e going to wait; we are

Will

1. a 'll/will go
   b 'll/will sail
   c won't come
   d Will (you) write
2. a are (we) going to do; 'll/will have
   b 'm going to meet; 'm going to visit

Present continuous for future

1. a 're travelling
   b 'm meeting
   c 're taking
   d are riding
   e 'm getting

Ability and possibility: can/could

1. a No, I couldn't. / No, we couldn't.
   b No, she couldn't.
   c Yes, they could.
   d Yes, he could.
2. a Can; can't; can
   b Can; can; couldn't
   c Could; could; couldn't

Obligation: have to/had to

1. a had to
   b don't have to
   c didn't have to
   d has to
2. a Do (you) have to
   b had to
   c has to
   d don't have to

Requests and permission: can, could, would

1. a Can
   b would like
   c can't

Present perfect

1. a 've camped
   b 's gone
   c 've seen
   d 's snowed
2. b She hasn't gone to Korea.

c They haven't seen the film.
d It hasn't snowed in the mountains.

3. a 's/has gone
   b Have (you) been
   c 've/have been
   d Has (she) gone
4. a Have you taken; haven't
   b Has she enjoyed; has
   c Have they read; they have
   d Has Jo spent; she hasn't
   e Have Ben and Lucy ridden; they have

Present perfect with ever and never

1. a Has she ever lost a competition?
   b Has he ever ridden a mountain bike?
   c Have you ever eaten an ice cube?
   d They've never seen tigers.

First conditional

1. a If you eat too much chocolate, you'll get stomach ache.
   b I'll eat your sandwich if you don't feel hungry.
   c If we hurry up, we won't be late for dinner.
   d I won't be upset if I don't get an award.
2. a it's
   b don't follow
   c 'll buy
   d doesn't finish
3. a start; will be
   b 'll/will have; doesn't rain
   c 'll/will be; don't have
   d will call; needs

Advice: should

1. a should (I) bake
   b should (I) bring
   c Should (we) grill
   d should (we) have
2. a should find
   b shouldn't be
   c should eat

d shouldn't go
e should make sure
f should drink

SPEAKING BANK

Section 10

1. a the past
   b things a person likes
   c the future
   d a thing, the future, things a person likes
   e things a person likes
   f a person
   g everyday life
   h everyday life, a place
2. Students' own answers.
3. 1 c, 2 a, 3 b, 4 d
4. Students' own answers.

Section 12

1–5 Students' own answers.

Section 13

1. a 2, b 3, c 5, d 1, e 4
2. a 4, b 1, c 2, d 5, e 3
3 & 4 Students' own answers.

WRITING BANK

Section 8

1. a Hi Belinda
   b All you need to do is register on our website and complete the form.
   c There is a question about the city you want to choose.
   d Hope to see you there!
2. a 3, b 5, c 4, d 2, e 1

Section 9

1. Students' own answers.
2. a terrible
   b interesting
   c badly
   d excited
   e cheap
3. Students' own answers.

ANSWER KEY

PAPER AND COMPUTER BASED TESTS

PTE General (otherwise known as *Pearson English International Certificate*) is widely accepted by hundreds of schools, universities and government bodies around the world. It is recognised as a test of language proficiency that measures real-world English skills and test taker's ability to use real language from everyday life. PTE General has until now only been available as a paper-based test. But as of Spring 2021, there will also be a computer-based version of the test available.

The Paper-Based Test

PTE General is a scenario-based English language test, designed to allow students the freedom to express themselves, show what they can do and how well they can use English. During the paper-based test, real-life tasks (such as writing messages, understanding talks and newspaper articles, or participating in conversation) assess a test taker's ability to perform everyday, familiar tasks in English.

Paper-based tests are available across all six levels of CEFR proficiency (A1, A2, B1, B2, C1 and C2) and can be taken by anyone over the age of 14 years old. The test is split into two parts: a written paper (which tests your skills in listening, reading and writing) and a speaking interview with an examiner (which test your speaking skills).

Test takers can take a paper-based test during one of the seven sessions available per year, at one of hundreds of authorised test centres around the world. The paper-based written and spoken parts of the test are both marked by UK examiners. PTE General test score reports are available within approximately four to six weeks, with test certificates awarded by Edexcel.

The Computer-Based Test

A computer-based version of the PTE General test is currently under development. Based on the solid foundations of the paper-based test, it retains many of the features that make PTE General a reliable and trusted English language test. However, it is also different to the paper-based test in several ways:

- **How to take the test.** The computer-based test will be entirely taken on a computer, assessing all four skills (including speaking skills). Test takers will use a keyboard to do the tasks and record speaking responses through a microphone.

- **When to take the test.** Test takers will be able to take the computer-based test on demand around the world, based on authorised test centre availability.

- **Integrated skills.** The paper-based version tests all four skills through separate sections within the written paper (listening, reading and writing) and a one-to-one oral test of speaking. The computer-based test combines integrated skill testing through different tasks, which may combine listening and writing, listening and speaking, or reading and writing.

- **Tasks in the test.** Digital tasks in the computer-based test allow testing of integrated four skills in an online format.

- **Scoring.** The paper-based test is marked by experienced examiners in the UK, whereas the computer-based test is scored by a secure and accurate automated scoring system. Score reports for the computer-based test are available within two weeks.

Comparison of PTE General Tests

Delivery	Computer-based Test	Paper-based Test
Length	Under 2 hours	1.5–3 hours
Levels	Standard format across six test levels in the test suite focused on CEFR levels (A1, A2, B1, B2, C1 and C2).	Standard format across six test levels in the test suite focused on CEFR levels (A1, A2, B1, B2, C1 and C2).
GSE and CEFR	All six levels test A1 to C2 on the Common European Framework. The tasks in the test have been created in line with the GSE scale, which will link into scoring in late 2021.	All four levels test A1 to C2 on the Common European Framework.
Language skills	Assesses all four skills (listening, reading, writing and speaking) through integrated digital tasks.	Assesses all four skills (listening, reading, writing and speaking) through tasks in a written paper and an oral test.
Task types	There are 12 task types in the test. All 12 task types integrate skills in English, across different kinds of digital tasks.	There are 12 task types in the test at A2 level. Three of the task types are part of the oral test.
Test delivery	The entire test is taken on a computer. Test will be available on demand based on test centre availability.	The test is split into a written paper (listening, reading and writing) and an oral speaking test. Tests are scheduled across seven sessions per year, at test centres.
Scoring	Computer-scored	Human marking
Score reports	Results will be available two weeks after taking the test. Score reports will show the level earned by the test taker as well as information on strengths, weaknesses and a recommended learning path.	Results are available five to eight weeks after taking the test. Score report shows the overall score and the skills scores.

For more information on the computer-based test:

 Go to **Student's Guide to the Computer Based Test** *on the* **Pearson English Portal**

Pearson Education Limited
KAO TWO
KAO Park
Hockham Way
Harlow, Essex
CM17 9SR
England

and Associated Companies throughout the world.

English.com/practicetestsplus

First published 2020

ISBN: 978-1-292-35340-1 (with key)

Set in Helvetica Neue LT WIG 10/12pt and Gill Sans 10/12pt

Printed and bound by Neografia, Slovakia

Acknowledgements
The Publishers and authors would like to thank the following people for their feedback and comments during the development of the material:
Irene Nardiello.

Picture Credits
The publisher would like to thank the following for their kind permission to reproduce their photographs:

123RF; mallinka, Roman Luka, **Pearson Education Ltd**; Anup John/Pearson India Education Services Pvt. Ltd, **Shutterstock**; Alexander Limbach, ahmad agung wijayanto, yayha, philia, Nagy Jozsef, Findriyani, Wiktoria Matynia, Skocko

Cover Images:
Getty Images: Tetra Images

Illustrated by:
Kevin Hopgood (Beehive Illustration) pp11-13, p28, p30, pp56-59, pp6-66, pp76-78, p85, pp96-98, pp104-106, pp116-118, pp124-126; John Batten (Beehive Illustration) p44, p57, p64, p78, p86, p91, p98, pp104-105, pp116-118, p155-159, p162; Joseph Wilkins (Beehive Illustration) pp12-13, p29, pp44, p57-59, p64, p71, pp76-78, p84, p91, pp96-98, p106, p111, pp117-118, pp124-126, p131; Mike Phillips (Beehive Illustration) p11, p56, p76, p96, p116.

All other images © Pearson Education

Other Credits
We are grateful to the following for permission to reproduce copyright material:

Video:
A Silversun Media Group and MW Photo-Video production for Pearson

Every effort has been made to trace the copyright holders and we apologise in advance for any unintentional omissions. We would be pleased to insert the appropriate acknowledgement in any subsequent edition of this publication.